GROSSET'S COMPLETE GUIDE
TO COLLECTIBLE PLATES

GROSSET'S COMPLETE GUIDE TO COLLECTIBLE PLATES

Hal L. Cohen

GROSSET & DUNLAP

Publishers   New York

To Polly, with love,
and Marie,
who taught me love of knowledge

"Defining Plates" and "The 11-Point Guide to Knowledgeable Plate Collecting" are reprinted from articles by David W. Armstrong and Reese Palley in the June 1973 issue of *Acquire* magazine. Copyright 1973 by the Acquire Publishing Co., Inc., 170 Fifth Avenue, New York, N. Y. 10010. Used by permission.

Cover photograph showing the first issue of the 1970 Norman Rockwell Christmas plate, "Bringing Home the Tree," courtesy The Franklin Mint.
Copyright © 1970 The Franklin Mint

Contents

ACKNOWLEDGMENTS

INTRODUCTION

I. *Defining Plates*   I

II. *11-Point Guide to Knowledgeable Plate Collecting*   4

III. *Plate Grading, Plate Pricing, and How to Use the Checklist*   9

IV. *How to Display and Hang Your Plates*   12

V. *The Collectible Plates*   15

VI. *The History of Silver, Porcelain, and Glass*   224

VII. *How a Limited Edition Silver Plate is Made*   231

VIII. *A Glossary of Collectible Plate Terms*   234

SPECIAL ACKNOWLEDGMENTS AND REFERENCE SOURCES   238

ACKNOWLEDGMENTS

A book as complex and comprehensive as this one requires the help, cooperation, and contributions of many individuals and organizations. To give recognition to these valuable sources, and to aid the reader in seeking further information on his own, I have listed at the end of this book the names and addresses of dealers, of plate sources (distributors, importers, producing companies), of trade missions and embassies, and of newspapers and magazines. All of these organizations helped, in one way or another, with this volume.

I also want to express special thanks and appreciation to individuals who gave generously of their time, materials, and experience. If anyone has not been included in these mentions, it is through oversight, not intent. First, to those people who helped with information about the plates:

Addams Family—Matthew F. Schmid, Caroline McCrory; *America House*—David R. Brown, Shirley M. Johnson; *America the Beautiful*—E. Ward Russell; *American Commemorative Council*—Alan Drey; *Anri*—Matthew F. Schmid; *Antique Trader*—E. A. Babka; *Arta*—Heio W. Reich; *Aynsley China*—J. R. Pitts

Bareuther, Bareuther/Murillo—Luella Powell, Jerry Pala; *Bayel*—George W. Ebeling; *Berlin*—Matthew F. Schmid; *Bing & Grøndahl*—Joan Doyle, Jorgen Sannung, Pat Owen, D. Levin

Capo-Di-Monte—Koscherak Bros.; *Collector's Creations*—J. Park Morton; *Count Agazzi*—Pamela Bowman

The Danbury Mint—W. Frank Zimmerman, Meta L. Schroeter, R. S. Fortin, J. A. Canfield; *Daum*—D. Stanley Corcoran, P. Cherisey; *Blue Delft*—H. Blumner; *Boch Frères Delft*—George W. Ebeling; *Royal Delft (De Porceleyne Fles)*—Ivan Glickman; *Dresden*—Heio W. Reich; *D'Arceau-Limoges*—Julia Connolly

Fenton Art Glass—Wilmer C. Fenton; *Juan Ferrandiz*—Matthew F. Schmid; *Alfonso Fontana/Creative World*—Lee Benson; *Fostoria*—David B. Dalzell, Jr.; *Franconia*—Don Doctorow; *The Franklin Mint*—David R. Brown, Shirley M. Johnson; *Frankoma*—John Frank; *Fürstenberg*—Heio W. Reich

The George Washington Mint/Medallic Art Company—Dianne L. Kekessy, Donald A. Schwartz, D. Davis; *Gorham Silver Company*—Ted Materna; *Greentree/Heritage*—Joan L. Zug; *Gunther Granget*—Barbara D. Gelinas

The Hamilton Mint—Tom Rubel; *Haviland & Co.*—Frederick Haviland; *Haviland & Parlon*—Lloyd J. Glasgow; *Hummel (Goebel)*—James P. Kelly; *Hummel (Schmid)*—Matthew F. Schmid, I. Weissman

Imperial Glass—Lucille Kennedy, C. E. Gustkey; *International Silver Company*—Cindy Haskins; *Israel Creations*—Michael Himelstein, I. Wolsky

Georg Jensen—Kermit Green, Lily Townsend, Judy Thornton

Kaiser—Pat Owen; *King's Porcelain*—Heio W. Reich; *Kirk Silver*—S. Kirk Millspaugh, Sandy Marcus, Pat Barber

Lalique—Lloyd Glasgow; *Lenox*—William E. Wedemeyer, Jr., Karen Cohen; *The Lincoln Mint*—Clay Donner; *Lund & Clausen*—Abel Abrahamsen *(Norsk)*

Kay Mallek—Kay Mallek; *Marmot*—Heio W. Reich; *Metawa*—Matthew F. Schmid; *Metlox*—Doug Bothwell; *Moser*—Heio W. Reich; *Mueller, Wuerful/Schmid*—Matthew F. Schmid

Nidaros—Abel Abrahamsen *(Norsk)*

Orrefors—Abel Abrahamsen *(Norsk)*

Peanuts—Matthew F. Schmid; *Pickard*—Henry A. Pickard; *Poillerat*—Paul Jokelson; *Poole Pottery, Ltd.*—B. H. Berman, W. J. Griffin, Randi Crystal; *Porsgrund*—Abel Abrahamsen, Hans Chr. Kontni *(Norsk); Puiforcat*—Anthony H. Clipper, A. E. Reiss

Reed & Barton—Stafford P. Osborn, Anne Silva; *Rorstrand*—Abel Abrahamsen *(Norsk); Rosenthal*—Peter Meltzer; *Royal Bayreuth*—Daniel M. Price, Bud Kern; *Royal Copenhagen*—Pat Owen, Birger Nordlund; *Royal Doulton*—Nancy E. O. Clarke, J. C. Geran; *Royal Irish Silver, Ltd.*—Peter H. Gunning; *Royal Tettau*—Daniel M. Price; *Royale/Germania Crystal*—Dorothy George

Schumann—George W. Ebeling; *Seven Seas Traders*—Sylvester A. Wetle; *Silver City*—Bud Kern; *L. E. Smith Glass/Wendell August Forge*—Hank Opperman, B. Shebeck; *Spode*—Christopher Church, Barbara Deutsch, L. R. Whiter; *Franz Stanek/Wara Intercontinental* —Luella Powell, W. A. Rautenberg; *Stumar*—Sid Sachs; *Svend-Jensen/Désirée*—Erik Larsen, H. C. Torbol

Val Saint Lambert—H. Schulte; *Veneto Flair/Creative World*—Lee Benson, Margie

Wedgwood—A. J. Pointon, Claudia Coleman; *The Wellings Mint*— David R. Brown, Shirley M. Johnson; *Wheaton/Nuline Glass*— John F. Heiner, C. W. Wagner; *Wilton Armetale*—Jack Fitzpatrick, L. D. Mulliner.

Second, I want to thank the following magazine editors and publishers for permission to use material from various issues: Robert Campbell Rowe of *Acquire;* Don Doctorow of *China Glass & Tablewares;* and April E. Martin of *Ltd. Editions Report.*

Third, for photographic work, thanks to *Topp Studios* at 225 Fifth Avenue, New York, N. Y. 10010; for permission to use photographs in the section on displaying and hanging plates, my thanks to Paul B. Roberts, *Roberts Colonial House*, 300 East 152nd Street, Harvey, Ill. 60426, and Elgin Thompson, *T & B Sales*, P. O. Box 248, Old Hickory, Tenn. 37138; and to *The Hamilton Mint* for the photographs in the section on how limited edition silver plates are made.

Finally, for help with the manuscript, my thanks to Jonathan Steinhoff, Joe Greene, Pat Sheenan, and Henry Krawitz. For invaluable assistance in every aspect of the creation and production of this book, my warmest thanks to Leslie Elliott.

Introduction

On the following pages are to be found the collectible plates issued by most of the plate creators, designers, and producers of the world.

Many of these plates are beautiful, artistic creations made in sterling silver, solid gold, crystal, glass, porcelain, majolica, and delftware. They have been designed by artists of international stature. World-famous porcelain, glass, and metal companies whose histories date back to royal charters issued in the Middle Ages have produced many of these fine items. A large number of the plates are mass produced, featuring popular themes tied in with a holiday or patriotic event.

As a recent phenomenon in the world of collecting, plates have weathered a cycle of "boom and bust" (1969–1972). Attempts to cash in on the success boom created by the early issues of The Franklin Mint, The Hamilton Mint, Lalique, Veneto Flair, Seven Seas, Count Agazzi, and others saw the proliferation of many "quickie" issues of limited artistic appeal and questionable status as limited edition collectible plates.

Those issues that have survived have done so on the strength of their artistic and creative appeal. The companies that presently produce these plates find that the market is healthy and receptive. Plates made of precious metals have also risen in intrinsic value due to the worldwide increase in the price of silver and gold. These plates should, however, be acquired primarily for their appeal as collectible pieces; the value of the metal content should remain a secondary consideration.

If any single bit of advice could be offered to the readers of this book, it would be: "Buy what you like and like what you buy."

Neither the author nor the publisher are in the collectible plate business. We do not buy, sell, or appraise these items. Our only desire is to inform and educate the interested reader in this fascinating subject. All prices contained herein are solely intended to serve as guidelines and are not warranted as to their accuracy.

I

Defining Plates

from an article by David W. Armstrong in ACQUIRE MAGAZINE

In the popular field of collector's plates, many traditional but loosely defined terms are sorely in need of redefinition. Their clarification through discussion and reevaluation will prove worthwhile to producers, collectors, and those individuals who are concerned with plate collecting.

One particularly gray area is that of the *limited edition*. The meaning of this term has become increasingly vague through overuse and the interpretations are legion. Yet it is one of the most important and prestigious designations in the collector's world. Some companies advocate that the term *limited edition* should be applied to any collector's plate. Yet many of these companies are unwilling to divulge the quantity of plates that they have produced within a year's time.

Collectors, on the other hand, seem to be searching for plates that are not only signed and dated but numbered. At the least, they demand to know how many plates in a particular edition will be released.

This brings to mind a rather humorous anecdote concerning the Bing & Grøndahl Company. Some time ago a collector asked one of the company's supervisors how many Christmas plates were produced each year. The supervisor replied that they employ a man whose duty it is to carefully count each plate during the entire year's production. When the last load of plates is placed in the kiln at the end of the year, this man is put in with them so that no one will ever know the exact quantity. The Bing and Grøndahl Company has produced in excess of 200,000 Christmas plates in recent years. In truth, this is far from a limited edition. Yet it *is* a collector's plate. In fact, the Bing & Grøndahl Christmas plates are collected in almost every country, which is more than can be said for most collector's plates.

Definitions of key terms follow.*

Collector's Plate—A plate whose production is confined to a particular year or period of time not to exceed one year. The plate must be dated and signed, or, in lieu of signature, must bear the stamp of the company that created it. Examples are the Bing & Grøndahl Christmas plates and the Royal Copenhagen Christmas plates.

Limited Edition—An edition of a particular plate not to exceed 10,000. It is my feeling that 10,000 is an adequate number of plates to be considered a limited edition. Any amount over this quantity is not really limited. In the past, manufacturers have tacked on the name "limited edition" to help sell plates whose edition was not really limited at all. The term has been misused and bandied about so much that it has actually hurt the collectors' market. Examples of limited edition plates are the Haviland-Parlon "Unicorn" series, the 1971 and 1972 Fuerstenberg plates, the 1971 and 1972 Dresden Christmas plates, and the Granget Christmas and Spring plates.

Numbered Edition—An edition in which each piece of the edition is individually numbered. The numbering is, in some cases, very difficult to accomplish. It is much more expensive for the manufacturer because of the labor involved and the time required to keep track of the individual numbers. However, it is a protective measure for the collector because it serves as the manufacturer's guarantee that only a specific number of the edition will be made; if two of the same numbers ever show up, the manufacturer is in trouble. A low number is not necessarily more valuable than a high number. It merely proves that it is a specific part of the numbered edition. In lithography, the first ten prints that are pulled are considered to be more valuable than the subsequent prints because they are personally examined by the artist; they are also slightly clearer than the subsequent editions. In most cases, this does not apply to collector's plates. However, the Number One piece of any edition seems to command a little more

* To look up other commonly used collectible plate terms, see the glossary.

2

value because of the prestige involved in owning it. Examples of numbered editions are the Hutschenreuther plates by John Ruthven and the Franklin Mint silver plates. It is interesting to note that the Franklin Mint plates would be defined as collector's plates, *not* limited editions, because the Franklin Mint consistently manufactures editions of over 10,000. They are, however, numbered editions.

Prime Numbered Editions—A limited edition of 2,000 plates or less. Examples of prime numbered editions are Pickard Game Bird plates and the Veneto Flair plates.

Why Buy Collectible Plates?

In seeking to clarify the familiar but cloudy terms used in plate collecting, it might be useful to reexamine the motives for collecting and producing collector's plates. A few important considerations for the collector might be:

1. *Buy for aesthetic appeal.* Buy the plates that you really like and would be happy to live with. If you buy a plate just because someone tells you that it has the potential for going up in value, dissatisfaction could quickly ensue should the plate not appreciate.

2. *Buy for design or theme.* The design on the plate should be well executed as well as appealing. If you purchase the plate for investment potential, the theme should be one that a large segment of collectors can identify with. If the theme is limited, the plate will cater only to a select group, thereby reducing the investment potential. For example, a Christmas plate would appeal to anyone, while a plate with your family's picture on it would have a very limited appeal, namely, for the members of your immediate household.

3. *Look for documentation.* One of the main reasons for the popularity of collector's plates is their excellent documentation. They can be dated, signed, and numbered. When we compare the collector's plate with other collector's items, this feature becomes a great advantage because it prevents reproductions from being made. Some plates even have certificates that accompany them, as well as a folder elaborating on the design of the plate.

Companies should also reevaluate their motives and priorities; their releases should hopefully be based on the integrity of the art objects which they produce.

II

11-Point Guide to Knowledgeable Plate Collecting

from an article by Reese Palley in ACQUIRE MAGAZINE

Before buying any plate, ask yourself these questions:

1. Is the plate beautiful?

This question is perhaps the most subjective of all the criteria listed. Yet it is one only you can decide. The plate must be visually pleasing—something you feel you can live with and will want to hold on to.

Plates will, in the future, depend more and more on the simple visual beauty that has been lacking up to now. If a plate pleases your sense of beauty, go on to the other considerations.

2. Does it have artistic input?

The finer the artist whose creation appears on the plate, the more likely this particular limited edition will increase in value. Statements by the producer claiming that the artist is well known are of little value. Your decision must be based upon whether the artist is recognized internationally and whether the art world takes the work of that artist seriously.

The physical material of the plate does contribute somewhat to its value, but the real test must be based on artistic input. The finer the artist, the more likely the value of the plate will increase.

3. *What is the reputation of the craftsman?*

Always consider the reputation of the producer. You must be sure he can be relied upon not to take advantage of an extra "run" or to inflate the prices of his product in trade magazines. If the plate is an annual, you must be assured that he will make the second, third, or fourth year of the limited edition. There is nothing more useless than an annual plate which ceases to be produced.

Once you have established the veracity of the producer, you will find that anything he makes is worth considering.

4. *Is the plate numbered?*

The plate under consideration must be individually, uniquely, indelibly, and serially numbered on each and every example of the total edition.

Unless a piece meets these numbering requirements, it is not a true limited edition. It is not sufficient for the producer to simply announce the total number; nor is it sufficient for a certificate to be included with the object. In limited edition plates, only the editions numbered in the correct manner will be worth owning.

5. *Was the size of the edition preannounced?*

Always check the preannouncement of the edition size. The producer must categorically state how many plates will be made and whether any more will ever be made. A so-called limited edition which is limited only by the number of objects that can be sold is no limited edition.

Always check the number of the artist's proofs, foundry proofs, and other examples which might be produced in addition to the numbered edition. It is possible for a manufacturer to preannounce an edition size of 10,000 numbered plates and then make 10,000 more which are unnumbered, marking them as artist's proofs. If you are offered an object which only indicates edition size, ask if proofs are going to be produced, and, if so, how many. You are entitled to know.

5

6. Is the edition size realistic?

Generally speaking, the larger the edition the less will be its value. If everything else is equal, the smaller the edition the more interesting it will become. Bear in mind, however, that to create a market an edition must meet at least 5,000 pieces. It should not exceed 10,000 pieces. If it does, there is a chance that the market will be glutted.

7. Is it American?

This country is so full of creative drive and energy that the great collectors' editions will be, and are being, produced here. Since Americans represent the majority of the collectors' market, you will no doubt be most comfortable with an American product.

If the plate is American, it is a plus. If it is not, it will have to be extremely desirable on other levels to enter into serious consideration.

8. Does it incorporate some imaginative technological feature?

Bas-relief or embossed plates that involve the use of precious metal combined directly with art are of far greater worth than, say, an etched plate. An image that is molded directly from a piece of sculpture is even better.

Ask your dealer if any new technological advances were used in producing the plate; the image may have been struck in a unique manner, or perhaps even double-struck—both on the obverse and reverse.

Such technological advances point the way to better and more imaginative uses of raw material. Unless the plate that is being offered incorporates a creative use of technology, you should question carefully the reason it is being made at all.

9. Is the offering real? Do I have the right of refusal?

Never buy a limited edition object unless you have actually seen an example or a photograph of it. Too many limited edition objects are offered "in concept," which means an artist's idea of what the object should look like.

If you must buy an object before you actually see it, make sure that the retailer gives you the right of refusal in the event you don't like it. Much of the value depends on the way the object actually feels in your hands. Always feel the object . . . note what kind of finish it has . . . what the weight is like . . . how it balances.

10. What is the dollar value content?

Some limited edition plates are fashioned from raw materials that have a basic value of their own. The porcelain in porcelain plates has little or no value; the bronze in a bronze plate is worth only a few cents; electroplate objects may have a value of fifteen cents; and the silver in a sterling silver plate may have a "melt-down" value of twenty-five dollars, although this value may rise with the escalation of the commodity value of sterling silver.

Dollarwise, silver is best. Of course solid gold is better, but terribly expensive. If you are ever offered a gold plate, buy it.

11. Would I buy it anyway?

The most important question—one about which you must be completely honest with yourself—is: "If the object I am looking at was *not* a limited object, was *not* made of valuable material, and did *not* have the possibility of increasing in value, would I buy it anyway?"

The ultimate value of any limited edition depends, to a great extent, on whether people would want to own it for its own sake. Consider the question carefully. Keep in mind the fact that if enough people desire an object, whether it is a limited edition or not, the increase in value of the object is assured.

There you have the eleven points you will need to objectively consider a limited edition object. These criteria will most likely develop into an accepted standard for limited edition objects. They are adhered to by the reputable dealer and producer—and will serve you well if you follow them.

A NOTE ABOUT
☞ REPRODUCTIONS AND FAKES ☜

Some of the rarest and most valuable of the collectible plates have been illegally reproduced; this practice will probably continue as long as people buy limited edition plates.

The best protection against acquiring a reproduction masquerading as an original is to buy only from a reputable dealer. *He has had many years of experience in the field and will be able to differentiate between the two. This does not mean that he cannot make an error. However, the chance that he will is slight. A reputable, ethical dealer will always stand behind what he sells.*

III

Plate Grading, Plate Pricing, and How to Use the Checklist

Grading

Most plates listed in this book are retail priced for mint condition. In order for the buyer or seller to properly evaluate a given plate, it is necessary to define what the terms *retail price* and *mint condition* actually mean. To provide a proper frame of reference, other grades and classifications should also be explained. Since many collectible plates are bought and sold in conditions other than mint, prices should be scaled down accordingly. Listed below are definitions for *mint condition* and lesser conditions plus the corresponding price reductions.

Mint (M) Complete; like new. Color bright and clean. No chips, cracks, scrapes, or wear. All markings and stamps on the back clear and clean. Box or holder, if issued with plate, in excellent condition. Any certificate, testimony, card, or parchment issued with plate should be like new. Where an engraved or printed copy of the plate's art motif is a part of the package, also like new.

Extra Fine (EF) All color clean and clear. Slight wear on rims and front. Gold or silver embellishments perfect. Certificate or printed copy in fine condition. Box or container missing. *Worth 10% less than listed retail price.*

Fine (F) Plate shows slight wear, but color is generally clear and bright. All designs complete but worn. Labels or certificate could be missing. Gold or silver embellishments perfect. No box or container. *Worth 15% less than listed retail price.*

Very Good (VG) Plate shows some wear; gold or silver slightly worn. Labels or certificate missing. No box or container. *Worth 25% less than listed retail price.*

Good (G) Plate shows wear. Design complete but color faded. Gold or silver shows wear. Labels, certificates, printed copies missing. No box or container. *Worth 40% less than listed retail price.*

Fair (FR) Color worn and gold or silver faded. Labels and certificates missing. Design complete but worn and faded. An undesirable category. No box or container. *Worth 50% to 75% less than listed retail price.*

Pricing—Retail and A.B.P.

The *retail price* is the amount you would have to pay an authorized dealer for a particular collectible plate. The retail prices in this book have been compiled from those supplied by plate manufacturers, producers, dealers, auction lists, catalogs, antique magazines, newspapers, and other authoritative publications. Retail prices are affected by a wide variety of factors: source, type of plate, number issued, designer, desirability, condition, and material used in producing the plate. The fluctuations in the price of silver and gold is a determining factor in the retail price of plates made from these materials. Combined with this is the fact that many plates are deliberately produced in limited quantities for special situations, without reissues. Given the above variables, these prices may jump abruptly at any time.

The *Average Buying Price* (A.B.P.) is the amount an authorized dealer *will pay you* for a particular collectible plate. Once an item is purchased from a dealer it disappears into a private home or collection and is permanently removed from the active market. As a consequence, dealers welcome people with genuine and desirable collectible plates to sell. We have given average buying prices for a few categories. However, where it has not been included in a category, a good rule of thumb would be to calculate the average buying price as 30–60% of the retail price. (Please keep in mind that a dealer in antiques and collectibles is a businessman, first and foremost, and must operate at a profit.) As a general rule, the more valuable the plate the higher the A.B.P. As with the retail price, the A.B.P. is contingent upon scarcity, condition, source, and desirability.

How to Use the Checklist

Appearing beside all listings is a check box. This will enable you to keep an accurate record of items which you own, or would like to own, as well as their condition. You may indicate the condition of an object by placing one of the following symbols in the check box.

⧅ "As found" ⧄ "Good" ⊟ "Fine" ⧆ "Excellent or Mint"

To the left of the check box, a simple cross will serve to remind you of an article that you would like to acquire, while a check mark will show that you already own it.

×□ "Want"   √□ "Have"

IV

How to Display and Hang Your Plates

Fine art forms should not be hidden away in vaults. They deserve to be displayed proudly for the pleasure and enrichment of family and friends.

Collectors often display their plates on walls, mantels, or tabletops. A plate improperly hung on a wall can fall off and break. To help you avoid this needless loss we offer the following advice: Don't use string; it can disintegrate. Don't use copper or aluminum wire or nails; these metals can corrode. We have found steel or brass to be the most dependable material. Remember that the nail must be struck well into the wall, with either a wire twisted through the back holes or a springer hanger attached.

Wooden plate frames protect and enhance any plate. They are produced in both round and square shapes and come in a variety of sizes and styles to fit plates of every dimension. Round frames are available in either fruitwood, antique white, antique black, or gold. Square frames come in fruitwood, walnut, and white. They can be purchased with glass fronts. Square frames convert a round plate into a more conventional picture-frame display and further protect the plate once it has been affixed to the wall. These frames can be used for plates with a diameter of from 5″ to 10½″. Plastic plate frames with red, blue, or green velvet backs are used for display of crystal plates.

Springer wall hanger

Wooden picture frame

Wooden plate easel

Wooden prop stand

Plate display rails designed for wall mounting can usually accommodate four to six plates. The rim of the plate is inserted in the rail with the plate resting against the wall.

Wooden plate easels are the simplest and cheapest way to display plates on a tabletop or other flat surface. They come in small, medium, and large sizes and can safely hold plates from 5″ to 12″ in diameter.

Twist-wire easels

Twist-wire stands

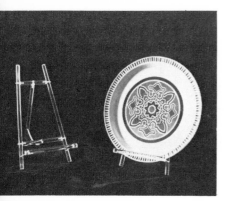

Clear plastic easels

Plexiglas stands

Adjustable plastic plate stands, which are also available in graduated sizes, perform the same function as the plate easels—they prop the plate up on a flat surface.

For overall display and long-term protection of your valuable plates, the wall variety of plate frames are highly recommended.

V

The Collectible Plates

The entries in this section are listed according to the name by which the plate or plate series is best known. This can be the name of the manufacturer (e.g., Bing & Grøndahl), the designer (e.g., Gunther Granget), the issuing organization or distributor (e.g., Veneto Flair), or the name the plate or series has been given (e.g., Addams Family). All Delft plates, regardless of name, are listed under "Delft." The country where the plate is produced appears in parentheses under the plate name.

Prices

All prices quoted are for plates in mint condition. These prices are approximate retail values at the time of publication. In many cases price ranges have been given. Prices for plates of silver and gold are subject to change due to the fluctuation in price of the metals. For an explanation of A.B.P. (Average Buying Price), which is referred to throughout the book, see page 10.

Neither the author nor the publisher are in the collectible plate field. We do not buy, sell, or appraise these items. Our only desire is to inform and educate the interested reader in this fascinating subject. All prices contained herein are solely intended to serve as guidelines and are not warranted as to their accuracy.

ADDAMS FAMILY

(Japan)

1

2

The theme for these two interesting limited edition plates is the humorous and popular cartoon "horror" family, The Addams Family, drawn by Charles Addams. Overglaze decoration is used on these porcelain plates.

Christmas Plate, 8"

1. ☐ 1972— FIRST ISSUE   CHRISTMAS DINNER   10.00*

Mother's Day Plate, 8"

2. ☐1972— FIRST ISSUE   ON THE TRACKS   10.00

* *Prices quoted in book are approximate retail for plates in mint condition. For explanation of A.B.P. (Average Buying Price) and Mint Condition see pages 9–11.*

16

AMERICA HOUSE/
THE FRANKLIN MINT
(U. S. A.)

A subsidiary of The Franklin Mint is responsible for this limited edition. Each plate is handmade of metal and designed in bas-relief. The deep-colored bronze plate has a strikingly rich appearance. The silver plate weighs a full seventeen ounces. Each plate is accompanied by a walnut and glass display case, a personalized certificate of authenticity, and the signature of the artist.

America House Plate, 8¾"

1972	LANDING OF COLUMBUS,	
☐	STERLING SILVER	200.00*
☐	BRONZE	100.00

* Prices quoted are approximate retail for plates in mint condition. Silver and gold plate prices subject to radical change due to price fluctuation of these metals. For explanation of A.B.P. (Average Buying Price) and Mint Condition see pages 9–11.

AMERICA THE BEAUTIFUL
(U. S. A.)

1

2

3

The America The Beautiful series of limited edition glass collector's plates commemorates well-known American landmarks and national shrines. Each plate in the series either illustrates a scene of natural beauty or one associated with American historic personages or events. The series was conceived, commissioned, and is distributed by E. Ward Russell of Silver Spring, Maryland, a suburb of Washington, D. C.

The current series of 10″ plates were produced by the Imperial Glass Corporation, Bellaire, Ohio, in a limited edition of less than 500. The Greek key border is retained each year. The back of the plate is marked with the America The Beautiful stamp, the Imperial Glass ("IG") trademark, and the plate's number in the series. The front of the plate bears the year and the subject. All are iridescent in the manner of carnival glass, reflecting yet another of Russell's interests; he is the founder of the American Carnival Glass Association, and is now president emeritus of that organization.

Two well-known sculptors have brought their artistic talents to the series, interpreting Russell's original designs and preparing them for the final process of making the mould in which the glass plate is to be pressed. The final product represents one of the most beautiful collector's plates ever produced in the United States.

America The Beautiful Plate, 10″

[For color illustrations, see page 171.]

1. ☐ 1969— FIRST ISSUE	U. S. CAPITOL,		
		RED CARNIVAL GLASS	25.00
		RED SATIN GLASS	30.00
2. ☐ 1970	MOUNT RUSHMORE,		
		GREEN CARNIVAL	20.00
3. ☐ 1971	STATUE OF LIBERTY,		
		AMBER CARNIVAL	20.00
4. ☐ 1972	MONUMENT VALLEY,		
		MARIGOLD CARNIVAL	20.00
5. ☐ 1973	LIBERTY BELL, WHITE		20.00

AMERICAN COMMEMORATIVE COUNCIL

(U. S. A.)

2

The American Commemorative Council and the National Historical Society have combined their talents to create and distribute an impressive collection of porcelain plates produced for them by the famous Gorham China Company.

The first plates to be issued are part of the Southern Landmark Series celebrating the historic southern homes and monuments where American history was made.

John Alan Maxwell, a native Virginian and a distinguished southern artist, has painted the full-color scenes reproduced on these plates. Each plate is separately fired four times and then rimmed in 24k gold. The issue number is limited to 9,800 pieces for each plate. Two plates are to be issued every year beginning with Monticello in 1973.

Southern Landmark Plate, 10½"

1. ☐ 1973	MONTICELLO	35.00
2. ☐ 1973	WILLIAMSBURG	35.00

ANRI

(Italy)

3   4   6

Hand-carved and hand-painted, these limited edition plates are designed by Spanish artist Juan Ferrandiz (who has his own line of plates listed separately in this book). They are produced in the part of Italy known as the Tyrol. Made of European maple, the best wood available for carving by master carvers and wood craftsmen, they possess a unique three-dimensional effect.

All issues are numbered and backstamped.

Christmas Plate, 12"

1. ☐ 1971— FIRST ISSUE	ST. JAKOB IN GRODEN	50.00–60.00
2. ☐ 1972	PIPERS AT ALBEROBELLO	35.00–45.00
3. ☐ 1973	HORNBLOWER—ZERMATT	50.00–100.00

Mother's Day Plate, 10"

4. ☐ 1972— FIRST ISSUE	MOTHER AND CHILDREN	35.00–40.00
5. ☐ 1973	MOTHER WITH BABY	40.00–45.00

Father's Day Plate, 10"

6. ☐ 1972— FIRST ISSUE	FATHER AND CHILDREN	35.00–40.00
7. ☐ 1973	FATHER PLAYING FIDDLE	30.00–40.00

ANTIQUE TRADER

(U. S. A.)

Christmas 1972   2

Mother's Day 1972   6

Antique Trader, one of the leading newspapers in the field of antiques and collectibles, commissioned this interesting and popular
group of limited edition plates. The plates are manufactured by the
Taylor-Smith & Taylor Company of East Liverpool, Ohio. E. A.
Babka, publisher of *Antique Trader*, has signed the back of these
plates, thus increasing their desirability. The plates are advertised
and sold in the pages of *Antique Trader*, as well as through other
outlets.

Issues of each edition range between 1,000–2,000 plates.

Christmas Plate, 8½"

1. ☐ 1971	CHRIST CHILD	15.00*
2. ☐ 1972	FLIGHT INTO EGYPT	15.00

Easter Plate, 8½"

3. ☐ 1971	CHILD AND LAMB	15.00
4. ☐ 1972	SHEPHERD WITH LAMB	15.00

Mother's Day Plate, 8½"

5. ☐ 1971	MADONNA AND CHILD	15.00
6. ☐ 1972	MOTHER CAT AND KITTENS	15.00

** Prices quoted in book are approximate retail for plates in mint condition. For explanation of
A.B.P. (Average Buying Price) and Mint Condition see pages 9–11.*

Father's Day Plate, 8½"

7. ☐ 1971	PILGRIM FATHER	15.00
8. ☐ 1972	DEER FAMILY	15.00

Thanksgiving Plate, 8½"

9. ☐ 1971	PILGRIM THANKSGIVING	15.00
10. ☐ 1972	THE FIRST THANKSGIVING	15.00

Bible Series, 8½"

11. ☐ 1973	DAVID AND GOLIATH	10.00
12. ☐ 1973	NOAH'S ARK	10.00

Charles M. Russell Plate, 8½"

[*For color illustrations, see page 173.*]

13. ☐ 1971— FIRST ISSUE DISCOVERY OF LAST CHANCE GULCH	12.50–15.00
14. ☐ 1971	A BAD ONE	12.50–15.00
15. ☐ 1971	INNOCENT ALLIES	12.50–15.00
16. ☐ 1971	A DOUBTFUL VISITOR	12.50–15.00

Currier & Ives Plate, 8½"

17. ☐ 1969	SET OF 4 PLATES	48.00
18. ☐ 1969	12" PLATTER (THE ROAD—WINTER)	17.50

Father's Day 1972   8

Thanksgiving 1972   10

ARTA

(Austria)

1   2

A beautiful item for admirers of enamelware is the 1973 Arta Christmas plate. It is produced in white enamel and bears a multicolored hand-painted nativity scene, charming in all its details. The nativity scene itself is surrounded by small angels, with the Star of Bethlehem shining over the crèche. The outer rim is dotted in red with a gold border. This edition is limited to 1,500.

A white enamel plate depicting a mother, her children, and their puppy is Arta's Mother's Day issue for 1973. The scene is delicately hand painted in several colors with a border of gold and red. The plate is issued in an edition of 1,500.

Christmas Plate, 7½"

1. ☐ 1973— FIRST ISSUE   NATIVITY SCENE: IN THE MANGER   50.00

Mother's Day Plate, 7½"

2. ☐ 1973— FIRST ISSUE   FAMILY SCENE WITH PUPPY   50.00

AYNSLEY CHINA

(England)

3

John Aynsley began his pottery business in the early 18th century. It was housed in his cottage in Staffordshire, England, the famous "Pottery District." By the 1860s Aynsley was producing fine bone china for Queen Victoria and other English notables.

In 1969 Aynsley produced the Prince of Wales Commemorative plate in a limited edition. The Aynsley Mayflower plate, made of bone china, was issued in 1970 to celebrate the 350th anniversary of the famous voyage. The Bath Abbey Commemorative plate was issued to celebrate one thousand years of English monarchy. In the year 973 A.D. the coronation of King Edgar took place at Bath Abbey, and for the first time in history the English nation was united in peace. The decoration consists of a very fine etching of the frontal view of Bath Abbey. The plate has been produced in a combination of black enamel and coin gold. The edition is limited to 1,000 pieces.

Commemorative Plate, 10½"

1. ☐	1969— FIRST ISSUE	PRINCE OF WALES	50.00
2. ☐	1970	MAYFLOWER	40.00
3. ☐	1973	BATH ABBEY—1000 YEARS	
		OF MONARCHY	25.00

BAREUTHER

(Germany)

3   4

The Bareuther porcelain factory was founded in 1867 by the German sculptor Johann Matthaeus Ries from Ottenlohe, Bavaria. His "factory" consisted of a small porcelain kiln and an annular brick kiln. Over the years, this small shop prospered and grew, eventually developing into a well-established industrial enterprise. The firm celebrated its centennial in 1967, and is now considered one of the leading porcelain factories.

In 1884 the founder's son, Johann Ries, sold the factory to Oskar Bareuther. At present, the factory employs approximately 700 people, including 60 painters and 60 printers. About half of the factory's production of dinnerware and giftware items are exported to more than thirty countries.

These limited edition plates are made of fine porcelain decorated in underglaze cobalt blue, and measure 8″. First issued in 1967 to celebrate the factory's hundredth anniversary, the Christmas plates depict typical Bavarian scenes. German paintings of the nineteenth and twentieth centuries are reproduced on the Mother's Day plates. The Father's Day plates feature German castles. A Thanksgiving series is also manufactured by Bareuther. Four non-limited edition plates containing reproductions in full color of seventeenth century paintings by Murillo (a Spanish artist known for his portraits of children and genre scenes) are also produced by Bareuther. These measure 11½″ in diameter.

Another limited edition series featuring famous Danish churches—consisting of midnight blue and underglaze plates—are also made by Bareuther. These plates were formerly called Roskilde church plates and are now sold under the name Danish Church plates. They should not be confused with Royal Copenhagen's Danish Cathedral series.

Christmas Plate, 8"

1. ☐ 1967— FIRST ISSUE	STIFSKIRCHE	75.00–100.00
2. ☐ 1968	KAPPELKIRCHE	12.50–20.00
3. ☐ 1969	CHRISTKINDLEMARKT	12.00–20.00
4. ☐ 1970	CHAPEL IN OBERNDORF	10.00–12.50
5. ☐ 1971	TOYS FOR SALE	10.00–12.50
6. ☐ 1972	CHRISTMAS IN MUNICH	15.00–27.00
7. ☐ 1973	CHRISTMAS SLEIGH RIDE	15.00–25.00

5   7

Mother's Day Plate, 8"

All are from paintings by Ludwig Richter

8. ☐ 1969— FIRST ISSUE	DANCING	35.00–50.00
9. ☐ 1970	MOTHER AND CHILDREN	16.00–20.00
10. ☐ 1971	DOING THE LAUNDRY	10.00–20.00
11. ☐ 1972	BABY'S FIRST STEP	14.50–25.00
12. ☐ 1973	MOTHER KISSING BABY	15.00–20.00

Father's Day Plate, 8"

All are from paintings by Hans Mueller

13. ☐ 1969—	FIRST ISSUE	CASTLE NEUSCHWANSTEIN	50.00–75.00
14. ☐ 1970		CASTLE PFALZ	16.00–20.00
15. ☐ 1971		CASTLE HEIDELBERG	10.00–15.00
16. ☐ 1972		CASTLE HOHENSCHWANGAU	14.50–17.50
17. ☐ 1973		CASTLE KATZ	14.50–17.50

Thanksgiving Day Plate, 8"

[For color illustrations, see page 66.]

18. ☐ 1971—	FIRST ISSUE	FIRST THANKSGIVING	15.00–20.00
19. ☐ 1972		HARVEST	14.50–16.50
20. ☐ 1973		COUNTRY ROAD IN AUTUMN	14.50–16.50

Danish Church Plate, 7¾"

21. ☐ 1968—	FIRST ISSUE	ROSKILDE CATHEDRAL	25.00
22. ☐ 1969		RIBE CATHEDRAL	17.50
23. ☐ 1970		MARMORKIRKEN	15.00
24. ☐ 1971		EJBY CHURCH	12.50
25. ☐ 1972		KALUNBORG KIRKE	13.00
26. ☐ 1973		GRUNDTVIG'S KIRKEN	13.00

Esteban Murillo Plate, 11½"

[For color illustrations, see page 66.]

27. ☐ 1972	BEGGAR BOYS PLAYING DICE	15.00
28. ☐ 1972	BOYS EATING MELONS AND GRAPES	15.00
29. ☐ 1972	FRUIT VENDORS COUNTING THEIR MONEY	15.00
30. ☐ 1972	BOYS EATING PASTRY	15.00

9

10

12

13

14

15

19

20

BAYEL

(France)

1

One of the oldest established glass producers in Europe, the Bayel Crystal Company has been making fine lead crystal products since 1666.

In 1972 they introduced a series of full lead crystal plates. The first issue depicted a delicately engraved rose in the center of the plate. The second issue featured an engraved orchid; the third featured lilies. Each edition is limited to 300 pieces. The plates are individually numbered and signed.

Bayel Annual Plate, 11"

---

1. ☐ 1972— FIRST ISSUE	ROSE		60.00*
2. ☐ 1973	ORCHID		50.00
3. ☐ 1973	LILIES		50.00

* Prices quoted in book are approximate retail for plates in mint condition. For explanation of A.B.P. (Average Buying Price) and Mint Condition see pages 9–11.

BELLEEK

(Ireland)

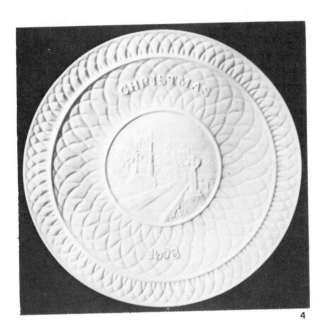

4

For many years Ireland's most respected and valuable porcelain has been produced by this company. Collectors everywhere recognize it. The porcelain is translucent and cream-colored. The Christmas plates, embossed with finely molded designs, are based on Irish subjects.

The plates are issued in editions of 5,000.

Christmas Plate, 7½"

1. ☐ 1970— FIRST ISSUE	CASTLE CALDWELL	125.00–175.00
2. ☐ 1971	CELTIC CROSS	30.00–40.00
3. ☐ 1972	FLIGHT OF THE EARLS	35.00–45.00
4. ☐ 1973	TRIBUTE TO W. B. YEATS	40.00–50.00

BERLIN DESIGN

(Germany)

Berlin Design plates are produced by the world-renowned 101-year-old Kaiser Alboth factory in Germany (whose Kaiser line is also listed in this book).

Decorated in underglaze cobalt blue and white, the limited edition plates from this factory measure 7½" in diameter. Festivities in German towns are pictured on their Christmas plates; the medieval churches and narrow streets form an appropriate setting. The Mother's Day plates depict animal mothers with their young. Episodes from American history are illustrated in the Father's Day series. Each Christmas plate issue ranges from 4,000–20,000; the Mother's and Father's Day issues range from 2,000–10,000.

In 1973, Berlin Design initiated a unique issue of plates illustrating subjects painted by Johannes Vermeer, the great Dutch painter of the seventeenth century. The editions are not annual issues, in the sense of being limited to one year's distribution, but are limited instead to a specific quantity of plates: each edition comprises only 3,000 numbered pieces. The plates measure 11½" in diameter, and are backstamped with the name of the painting, the total number of the edition, and the actual number of the plate. A certificate of authenticity signed by the managing director of the Kaiser factory is enclosed with each plate. The special process of cobalt underglaze blue magnificently enhances these famous subjects.

Christmas Plate, 7½"

[For color illustrations, see page 168.]

1. ☐ 1970— FIRST ISSUE	CHRISTMAS IN BERNKASTEL	45.00–100.00*
2. ☐ 1971	CHRISTMAS IN ROTHENBURG	12.50–15.00
3. ☐ 1972	CHRISTMAS IN MICHELSTADT	15.00–20.00
4. ☐ 1973	CHRISTMAS EVE AT WENDELSTEIN	15.00–20.00

---

* Prices quoted in book are approximate retail for plates in mint condition. For explanation of A.B.P. (Average Buying Price) and Mint Condition see pages 9–11.

5. ☐ 1971— FIRST ISSUE POODLES		18.50–20.00
6. ☐ 1972	FLEDGLINGS	12.00–15.00
7. ☐ 1973	THE DUCK FAMILY	25.00–40.00

3

4

6

7

33

Father's Day Plate 7½"

8. ☐ 1971— FIRST ISSUE BROOKLYN BRIDGE ON
                              OPENING DAY   17.50–20.00
9. ☐ 1972   THE CONTINENT SPANNED   12.50–15.00
10. ☐ 1973   LANDING OF COLUMBUS   18.00–20.00

Commemorative Plate, 7½"

11. ☐ 1972   OLYMPIADE MÜNCHEN   15.00

Johannes Vermeer Plate, 11½"

[For color illustrations, see page 168.]

12. ☐ 1973— FIRST ISSUE THE GEOGRAPHER   100.00
13. ☐ 1973   GIRL WITH LETTER   120.00
14. ☐ 1973   THE MILKMAID   120.00

8   9   10

12   13

BING & GRØNDAHL

(Denmark)

The firm of Bing & Grøndahl was established in 1853, but it was not until 1895 that Harald Bing introduced the world's first Christmas plate, created in the new underglaze technique.

The Bing & Grøndahl trademark is taken from the Three Towers on the coat of arms of the city of Copenhagen. The plates tell the story of Denmark and its people—their accomplishments, conquests, and way of life—and depict moods of joy, happiness, sorrow, and love. The fact that each Christmas plate is immediately sold out demonstrates the vivid interest displayed in these specimens of Danish design and craft. Through a world-wide network of distributors, devoted collectors look forward to receiving the annual addition to their cherished collection.

Very few people, however, own a complete collection. Not only are the earlier Christmas plates virtually impossible to acquire, but the new ones soon become highly cherished rarities. The number of Christmas plates produced is always controlled and limited; the molds are destroyed immediately after the production run is completed.

The Christmas plate mold is shaped by hand. One mold can be used approximately 20–25 times. Each molded plate is checked carefully for imperfections. Only perfect specimens are used for the first (twenty hour) firing. Only first quality plates are released from the factory. All plates are hand-painted on Copenhagen blue underglaze porcelain. The Bing & Grøndahl Christmas plate was the first in the world to be made with porcelain, and is considered by all collectors to be the original.

From 1903 to 1945 approximately 10,000–15,000 plates were produced for each year's Christmas plate issue. From 1946 to 1950, 25,000 per year; 1951 to 1956, 75,000; 1957 to 1962, 100,000; 1963 to 1969, 150,000; 1970 to present, 200,000. A complete set of B & G Christmas plates (1895–1973) would have a retail value of $8,750–$10,000. Complete sets in mint condition are very rare.

Notes on other Bing & Grøndahl plates accompany their listings further along in the text.

Christmas Plate, 7¼"

The approximate retail price for each plate is listed beside its year of issue.

☐ 1895   2750.00

☐ 1896   1550.00

☐ 1897   1000.00

☐ 1898   625.00

☐ 1899   1050.00

☐ 1900   650.00

☐ 1901   325.00

☐ 1902   250.00

☐ 1903   225.00

☐ 1904   110.00

☐ 1905   100.00

☐ 1906   90.00

☐ 1907   120.00

☐ 1908 70.00   ☐ 1909 85.00

☐ 1910 80.00   ☐ 1911 82.50   ☐ 1912 75.00

☐ 1913 75.00   ☐ 1914 65.00   ☐ 1915 100.00

☐ 1916 70.00   ☐ 1917 70.00   ☐ 1918 70.00

☐ 1919 72.50   ☐ 1920 62.50   ☐ 1921 62.50

☐ 1922   60.00   ☐ 1923   60.00

☐ 1924   65.00   ☐ 1925   60.00   ☐ 1926   60.00

☐ 1927   75.00   ☐ 1928   60.00   ☐ 1929   75.00

☐ 1930   85.00   ☐ 1931   65.00   ☐ 1932   75.00

☐ 1933   60.00   ☐ 1934   60.00

☐ 1935   60.00   ☐ 1936   70.00

☐ 1937   75.00   ☐ 1938   125.00   ☐ 1939   145.00

☐ 1940   145.00   ☐ 1941   280.00   ☐ 1942   145.00

☐ 1943   140.00   ☐ 1944   100.00   ☐ 1945   135.00

☐ 1946   65.00   ☐ 1947   90.00

☐ 1948   60.00   ☐ 1949   60.00

☐ 1950   90.00   ☐ 1951   65.00   ☐ 1952   55.00

☐ 1953   62.50   ☐ 1954   80.00   ☐ 1955   80.00

☐ 1956   126.00   ☐ 1957   126.00   ☐ 1958   96.00

40

☐ 1959   130.00   ☐ 1960   160.00

☐ 1961   72.50   ☐ 1962   50.00

☐ 1963   110.00   ☐ 1964   55.00   ☐ 1965   55.00

☐ 1966   50.00   ☐ 1967   35.00   ☐ 1968   35.00

☐ 1969   25.00   ☐ 1970   25.00   ☐ 1971   21.00

☐ 1972   21.00   ☐ 1973   28.00

41

The first Jubilee Plate was released by Bing & Grøndahl in 1915. It was a 9" diameter replica of the original 1895 (7¼") Christmas plate. Jubilee plates are issued every five years, and each 9" plate is a replica of one of the earlier Christmas plates. Listed below is the year of issue for each Jubilee plate as well as the year in which the original Christmas plate was produced.

☐ 1915— FIRST ISSUE—1895 PLATE	125.00
☐ 1920—1900 PLATE	105.00
☐ 1925—1915 PLATE	125.00
☐ 1930—1910 PLATE	225.00
☐ 1935—1907 PLATE	700.00
☐ 1940—1901 PLATE	1650.00
☐ 1945—1936 PLATE	325.00
☐ 1950—1928 PLATE	185.00
☐ 1955—1947 PLATE	175.00
☐ 1960—1950 PLATE	135.00
☐ 1965—1926 PLATE	85.00
☐ 1970—1914 PLATE	25.00

Easter Plaque, 7½"

From 1910 through 1935, Bing & Grøndahl produced Easter plaques in limited quantities. Their value has risen in recent years.

☐ 1910— FIRST ISSUE	50.00	☐ 1924	55.00
☐ 1911	50.00	☐ 1925	55.00
☐ 1912	60.00	☐ 1926	75.00
☐ 1913	60.00	☐ 1927	75.00
☐ 1914	60.00	☐ 1928	80.00
☐ 1915	55.00	☐ 1929	110.00
☐ 1916	55.00	☐ 1930	140.00
☐ 1917	60.00	☐ 1931	200.00
☐ 1918	55.00	☐ 1932	140.00
☐ 1920	55.00	☐ 1933	200.00
☐ 1921	55.00	☐ 1934	400.00
☐ 1922	65.00	☐ 1935	700.00
☐ 1923	55.00		

Bing & Grøndahl issued its first Mother's Day plate in 1969. These limited edition plates are hand-painted on Copenhagen blue underglaze porcelain.

1.	☐ 1969— FIRST ISSUE	DOG AND PUPPIES	275.00
2.	☐ 1970	BIRD AND CHICKS	35.00
3.	☐ 1971	CAT AND KITTENS	15.00
4.	☐ 1972	MARE AND FOAL	13.50
5.	☐ 1973	DUCK AND DUCKLINGS	15.00

Commemorative Plate

6.	☐ 1970	LIBERATION PLATE, 9"	30.00
7.	☐ 1971	REBILD PLATE, 6"	12.50
8.	☐ 1972	800TH BIRTHDAY PLATE, 6"	13.50
9.	☐ 1972	GREENLAND PLATE, 6"	12.50
10.	☐ 1972	OLYMPIAD PLATE, 7"	20.00
11.	☐ 1972	FREDERICK IX PLATE, 9"	50.00

5

11

BOEHM
(U. S. A.)

For the Edward Marshall Boehm plates, see *Lenox*.

BONITA
(Mexico)

Each sterling silver plate is individually numbered, affixed with the Mexican eagle hallmark of silver purity, and packed with a numbered certificate. Each plate is also hand-engraved by a team consisting of Raul Anguiano, a world-famous Mexican artist, two of his country's foremost engravers, and the silversmith who founded Mexico City's "Margo de Mexico" studio. The silver, which is of the highest quality, is signed by Anguiano and engraver Miguel Rios. The sterling silver they produce stands out as a superb work of art. The Mother's Day plate was limited to 4,000.

Mother's Day Plate

☐ 1972— FIRST ISSUE   MOTHER WITH BABY   75.00–125.00*

* *Prices quoted are approximate retail for plates in mint condition. Silver and gold plate prices subject to radical change due to price fluctuation of these metals. For explanation of A.B.P. (Average Buying Price) and Mint Condition see pages 9–11.*

CAPO-DI-MONTE

(Italy)

1

For hundreds of years the Italian porcelain company of Capo-Di-Monte has been a leader in the field of artistic ceramics.

The elaborate, embellished, baroque style typical of Capo-Di-Monte ceramics has been applied to the production of modern Christmas and Mother's Day plates.

Hand-painted cherubs in high relief, flowers, holly borders, gilding, and banding are all featured in these plates.

These are true limited edition plates—Christmas plates are restricted to 1,000 each, Mother's Day plates are limited to 500 each.

Christmas Plate, 7½"

1. ☐ 1972— FIRST ISSUE	HOLLY AND CHERUBS		125.00
2. ☐ 1973	BELLS AND HOLLY		60.00

Mother's Day Plate, 7½"

3. ☐ 1973— FIRST ISSUE	MOTHER AND CHILDREN		60.00

COLLECTOR'S CREATIONS
(U. S. A.)

1   2

Produced by one of America's finest silversmiths, these limited edition plates, truly works of fine art, are made in a unique combination of bronze, pure silver, and copper. Each edition is limited to 750 individually numbered pieces.

"Alice in Wonderland," the subject of the first issue, is based upon the famous hundred-year-old drawings of John Tenniel for Lewis Carroll's masterpiece.

"Christmas, by Thomas Nast," a first annual Christmas plate, features the jovial figure of Santa Claus created by Thomas Nast in the late 1800s. His charming interpretation has earned him the reputation of "the artist who made Santa Claus."

Christmas Plate, 11"
---

1. ☐ 1973— FIRST ISSUE THOMAS NAST'S *Christmas*   100.00–150.00*

John Tenniel's "Alice in Wonderland" Plate, 11"

[For color illustrations, see page 60.]

2. ☐ 1973— FIRST ISSUE ALICE IN WONDERLAND   100.00–150.00

   * *Prices quoted are approximate retail for plates in mint condition. Silver and gold plate prices subject to radical change due to price fluctuation of these metals. For explanation of A.B.P. (Average Buying Price) and Mint Condition see pages 9–11.*

COUNT AGAZZI

(U. S. A.)

2   4

Count Angelo Agazzi, the well-known Venetian artist, has hand-painted and signed each of these limited edition plates of imported Venetian glass. An almost iridescent quality is produced by the technique used to paint the reverse sides. The "Children's Hour," limited to editions of 2,000, was created for children, but appeals to people of all ages. The series features colorful pictures of fish, birds, and animals. Adorable angels in various positions are featured in the Easter Cherubs series, limited to 600 each. A realistic picture of the first step ever taken by a human being on the surface of the moon appears on the Apollo 11 plate, limited to an issue of 1,000. The "Famous Personalities" issue ranges from 500–1,000.

Children's Hour Plate, 6"

1. ☐ 1970— FIRST ISSUE	OWL		10.00–15.00
2. ☐ 1971	CAT		10.00–15.00
3. ☐ 1972	PONY		12.00–17.50
4. ☐ 1973	PANDA		12.00–15.00

Commemorative Plate, 10"

5. ☐ 1969	APOLLO 11—LUNAR LANDING	20.00–30.00

Easter Cherubs Plate, 10"

6. ☐ 1971—	FIRST ISSUE	PLAYING THE VIOLIN	10.00–20.00
7. ☐ 1972		AT PRAYER	10.00–20.00
8. ☐ 1973		WINGED CHERUB	10.00–20.00

Famous Personalities Plate, 7"

9. ☐ 1968—	FIRST ISSUE	NOTABLE PORTRAITS	25.00–40.00
10. ☐ 1970		NOTABLE PORTRAITS	15.00–20.00

Israeli Anniversary Plate, 10"

11. ☐ 1973	TOWER OF DAVID	15.00–30.00

Peace Plate, 6"

[For color illustrations, see page 167.]

12. ☐ 1973	GENERATION OF PEACE	10.00–15.00

7

9

12

CROWN STAFFORDSHIRE

(England)

Fine English bone china, featuring beautifully hand-painted flowers in soft and vibrant pastel colors, are typical of the products of this renowned Staffordshire porcelain factory. Designs are produced in low relief on the Christmas and Mother's Day plates.

Christmas Plate, 8"

1. ☐ 1972— FIRST ISSUE	POINSETTIA		30.00
2. ☐ 1973	CHRISTMAS ROSE		30.00

Mother's Day Plate, 8"

3. ☐ 1973— FIRST ISSUE	PEACE ROSE	30.00

THE DANBURY MINT
(U. S. A.)

The Danbury Mint is a private mint located in Westport, Connecticut. It issues unique, limited edition plates of sterling silver inlaid with 24k gold and burnished copper. Reed & Barton, one of the oldest and finest silversmiths in the United States, produces these plates for the Danbury Mint.

A series based on the works of Michelangelo began with the artist's painting of the *Creation*, located on the ceiling of the Sistine Chapel in Rome. Reproduced on a plate in bas-relief, it is composed of sterling silver, 24k gold, and copper. The plate contains twelve ounces of sterling silver. All plates in the series are produced in this manner. Each plate is limited to an edition of 7,500 pieces.

The well-known Currier & Ives lithographs also appear in a series. The first, issued in 1972, is entitled "The Road—Winter"; it depicts a happy couple in a horse-drawn sleigh. A second, produced in 1973, is entitled "The Skating Pond"; it portrays a winter scene in Central Park before the turn of the century. Both Currier & Ives plates are made of sterling silver with gold and copper inlays. Each plate is issued in a quantity of 7,500 pieces.

The American Bicentennial plates were issued to commemorate the forthcoming 200th anniversary of the founding of the United States. Scenes from famous events leading up to the Revolutionary War as well as scenes based upon the creation of the Declaration of Independence are etched on the sterling silver surface of the plates. One plate a year will be produced until 1976. The plates contain eight ounces of sterling silver. They are issued in quantities of 7,500 per issue.

Michelangelo Plate, 9"

1. ☐ 1972	THE CREATION OF ADAM	175.00*	
2. ☐ 1972	THE PIETÀ	125.00–175.00	
3. ☐ 1973	MOSES	125.00–175.00	

* *Prices quoted are approximate retail for plates in mint condition. Silver and gold plate prices subject to radical change due to price fluctuation of these metals. For explanation of A.B.P. (Average Buying Price) and Mint Condition see pages 9–11.*

Currier & Ives Plate, 8"

[For color illustrations, see page 60.]

4. ☐ 1972— FIRST ISSUE THE ROAD—WINTER   125.00–175.00
5. ☐ 1973   CENTRAL PARK—WINTER   125.00–175.00

Bicentennial Plate, 8"

6. ☐ 1972   1773—THE BOSTON TEA PARTY 125.00–175.00
7. ☐ 1973   1774—THE CONTINENTAL
                             CONGRESS   125.00–175.00

1   2

4   6

D'ARCEAU-LIMOGES
(France)

Fine french porcelain is the material used for the historic and unique Lafayette Legacy Collection, a subscription-only (not available from dealers) series of six beautiful Limoges plates. They illustrate scenes from the life of the Marquis de Lafayette, the French nobleman and hero of the American Revolution, who is also a national hero in France. Created from original art executed and signed by André Restieau, the plates are made in the finest porcelain by D'Arceau-Limoges, one of the foremost producers of the delicate, translucent Limoges "china." Each plate is individually numbered, registered, and has a Certificate of Origin, and the series is to be completed in time for the American bicentennial in 1976. The series is distributed in North America by Bradford Galleries Exchange.

Lafayette Legacy Plate, 8½"

1. ☐ 1973— FIRST ISSUE	LAFAYETTE ENLISTS IN THE REVOLUTIONARY ARMY	12.00–35.00
2. ☐ 1973	LAFAYETTE LANDS IN SOUTH CAROLINA	17.00–25.00

1

DAUM
(France)

5   6

The technique used on the Daum plates is called *pâte de verre*. This rare and ancient technique of crystal-making was used as far back as 3500 B.C. Specimens from 1500 B.C. have been found in the tomb of Pharaoh Amenhotep. The reproductive technique has nothing in common with the blowpipe method now used by crystal manufacturers all over the world. This technique is so difficult to acquire that, in the whole history of crystal-making, very few artisans have been known to practice it. Daum, after a few preliminary trials in 1905, and after years of painstaking research, has finally brought this technique up to date. The company was attracted by the marvelous possibilities of *pâte de verre* as a vehicle for creative artists in glass and plates.

The "Four Seasons" plates are made in *pâte de verre*. The design on each plate is by Raymond Corbin, famous French artist of the Paris Mint. It is executed in relief; as light passes through the plate it highlights the design, thus making the plate even more beautiful. Since the plates can only be purchased in sets of four, the numbers on all four plates are the same.

The Dali plates were created by Salvador Dali in 1971 exclusively for Daum. The extreme originality of this series lies in the fact that complementary designs on each plate correspond exactly to the surrealistic imagination of Dali. This is the reason why these plates can only be purchased in sets of two. The number is also engraved on each plate next to the Daum signature. Each set is sold in a fine box containing a certificate. They are also limited to 2,000 pieces for each design.

The "Musicians" series is made in clear crystal. The medallion in the center of the plate is in colored *pâte de verre*.

Four Seasons Plate, 10¼"

1. ☐ 1969	AUTUMN, AMETHYST	
2. ☐ 1970	WINTER, AQUAMARINE	Set of 4
3. ☐ 1970	SPRING, EMERALD	550.00–650.00
4. ☐ 1970	SUMMER, TOPAZ	

Dali Plate, 10¼"

[For color illustrations, see page 65.]

5. ☐ 1971	TRIOMPHALE, BLUE *pâte de verre* DECORATED WITH GOLD	Set of 2
6. ☐ 1971	CECI N'EST PAS UNE ASSIETTE, MAUVE *pâte de verre* DECORATED WITH GOLD	250.00–450.00

Musicians Plate, 10¼"

[For color illustrations, see page 65.]

7. ☐ 1970	BEETHOVEN, AMETHYST MEDALLION	60.00–80.00 Each
8. ☐ 1970	BACH, EMERALD (GREEN)	
9. ☐ 1971	MOZART, TOURMALINE (LIGHT BLUE)	
10. ☐ 1971	WAGNER, PERIDOT (YELLOW)	
11. ☐ 1972	GERSHWIN, SAPPHIRE (DARK BLUE)	

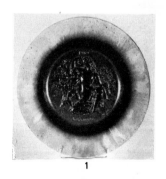

1

About Delft

The word "delft," which includes Dutch, German, Belgian, and Italian faience, originally referred only to the faience of the Netherlands. The industry dates back to the fourteenth century. The Dutch city of Delft was one of the major centers of production. There are now three major delft companies producing plates in limited editions.

Delft, a type of earthenware, is generally covered with a thin glaze. Although it is usually decorated with cobalt blue covers, it is also produced in shades of brown, green, black, sepia, red, and yellow. It can also be varicolored.

De Porceleyne Fles ("The Porcelain Flask"), also called the Royal Delft Company, has produced delftware of all types for over 300 years, making it the oldest company in existence. No two of their limited edition plates are alike, for each plate is hand-painted and signed by an artist at the factory. The Royal Delft Company is also known for its hand-painted decorative and artware pieces.

Blue Delft, also referred to as Schoonhaven, have been producing delftware for centuries. They began producing Christmas tiles in 1967. In 1970 a matching Christmas plate and spoon were introduced. These items were added to their Father's and Mother's Day tiles in 1971. Christmas items from France and Germany are also being offered now by Blue Delft.

Boch Frères Delft produces many different wares in an old-world style well suited for the reproduction of master engravings.

Another company which produces delftware (not listed in this volume) is Crown Delft, or V. K. Delfts. This firm issues Father's Day, Mother's Day, and *Kerstmis* plates. The Father's and Mother's Day plates were first issued in 1970; the first *Kerstmis* plate was made in 1969. They also make tiles whose history is identical with that of the plates.

The 1973 Blue Delft Christmas tile and Christmas plate, illustrating the relationship between the traditional tiles of Delft and the limited edition collectible plates they have inspired.

BLUE DELFT

(Holland)

Blue Delft represents the oldest and one of the best known ceramics in the world. The first Delft was inspired by Chinese blue and white stoneware, items which had become very popular on the European continent. The Dutch adaptations grew into a prosperous industry housed in defunct breweries in the town of Delft—the place from which the ceramic gets its name.

Delft reached its first popularity peak in the period between the seventeenth and eighteenth centuries. It became a favorite among European nobility and art collectors. In fact, one of the best-known art dealers today, The House of Duveen, began its operations in Delft. Delft was also indirectly responsible for the creation of Dresden and Meissenware; Dutch potters had migrated to Germany with the idea of imitating Delft.

Although early Delft was blue and white, red décor gained much favor in the nineteenth century. The Blue Delft Company recently revived this color as a concession to current tastes in American home decoration.

Like all art forms, Delft changed with the times and gradually acquired characteristics closer in spirit to its native Holland. The original oriental scenes were replaced by floral designs inspired by the beauty of Dutch flower fields; familiar windmill scenes were put to frequent use. Dutch designers created many new pieces in the unique Dutch style. In the Blue Delft collection alone there are more than 1,000 different pieces.

All decorating is done entirely by hand. At Schoonhaven's quaint Delft factory, built from the ruins of a medieval church, the artwork is done by skilled craftsmen who were taught the trade by their fathers. The craft is kept in the family and passed on to each succeeding generation.

Christmas Plate, 6½"

1. ☐ 1970— FIRST ISSUE	DRAWBRIDGE NEAR BINNENHOF		15.00
2. ☐ 1971	ST. LAURENS CHURCH		11.00
3. ☐ 1972	CHURCH AT BIERKADE, AMSTERDAM		12.00
4. ☐ 1973	CHRISTMAS PLATE		12.00

2

3

Mother's Day Plate, 6½"

5. ☐ 1971 —FIRST ISSUE MOTHER AND DAUGHTER
   OF THE 1600S   13.50
6. ☐ 1972   MOTHER AND DAUGHTER
   OF THE ISLE OF URK   12.00
7. ☐ 1973   REMBRANDT'S MOTHER   12.00

Father's Day Plate, 6½"

8. ☐ 1971— FIRST ISSUE FRANCESCO LANA'S AIRSHIP   10.00
9. ☐ 1972   DR. JONATHAN'S BALLOON   12.00

Olympic Plate, 6½"

10. ☐ 1972   OLYMPIC TORCH AND
    SYMBOL, MÜNCHEN   15.00–20.00

6

7

9

10

The Resurrection, above, and *Horizons West*, below, from
The Franklin Mint. © 1972, 1973 The Franklin Mint

Currier & Ives' *Central Park—Winter,* The Danbury Mint, 1973

Tenniel's *Alice in Wonderland,* Collector's Creations, 1973

We Three Kings
Reed & Barton, 1971

Rose de Noël
Gilbert Poillerat, 1973

A Partridge in a Pear Tree
Imperial Glass, 1970

Holy King Caspar
Rosenthal, 1972

Boehm's *Raccoons*
© 1973 Lenox, Inc.

The Burning of the Gaspee 1772
© 1972 Haviland & Co., Inc.

The Shoemaker (1973), left, and *Madonna of the Goldfinch* (1972), right, Fenton Art Glass

Left, *Angel in a Christmas Setting*
© 1971 W. Goebel (GmbH),
below, *Playing Hooky*, © 1973
Schmid Mngt.

Tulips
Royale/Germania Crystal, 1973

Sunbonnet Babies, left, and *Bavarian Village with Bridge*, right, Royal Bayreuth, 1973

Christmas 1971, above, and
Mother's Day 1971, right
Royal Copenhagen

Christmas 1970, 1971, 1972
(bottom to top)
Svend-Jensen/Désirée

*Christmas, Deluxe Christmas,
Mother's Day, Father's Day*
plates and mugs
Porsgrund, 1973

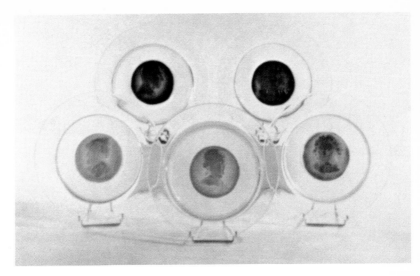

Above, Daum's *Musicians Series* (1970–72); Dali's *Ceci N'est Pas Une Assiette*, left, and *Triomphale*, below, both Daum 1971

Left, *The First Thanksgiving* (1971) and right, top to bottom, Murillo's *Boys Eating Melons and Grapes, Fruit Vendors Counting their Money,* and *Beggar Boys Playing Dice,* 1972, Bareuther

Colette and Child
Royal Doulton, 1973

BOCH FRÈRES DELFT

(Belgium)

2   1

The designs produced by this lesser-known but high-quality company are executed in rich shades of blue. Since they are taken from prints of master engravings, they are more like fine paintings than porcelain. Collectors everywhere are proud to display items made by this company, even though these objects are non-limited.

Boch Frères Delft Plate

[For color illustrations, see page 172.]

1. ☐ 1971	OLD LADY READING, 9¾"		8.50
2. ☐ 1971	FISHERMAN, 9¾"		8.50
3. ☐ 1972	CARRIAGE RIDE, 15½"		19.50
4. ☐ 1972	SLEIGH RIDE, 15½"		19.50

ROYAL DELFT
(DE PORCELEYNE FLES)
(Holland)

These handsome porcelain pieces portray the charm and beauty of Holland with great sensitivity. For the first time in their 320-year history De Porceleyne Fles has reproduced limited edition plates from two of their most prized antique delft tableware sets. The first issue, done in the Pijnacker style, is the Valentine's Day plate. Adrian Pijnacker, the artist after whom this 300-year-old set is named, was a pioneer in the use of pure gold on china. Rich blues, reds, and pure gold are hand-painted onto the white surface of the 7″ plate. The second issue, the 10″ Easter plate, is adapted from a 1653 design; it is part of Royal Delft's polychrome group, as distinguished from the blue designs. Produced in exquisite shades of rust, gold, green, and white on raised relief, it illustrates the old Dutch Easter cross tradition wherein children place bread baked in the shape of doves of peace on the points of the crosses, and then cover them with palm leaves.

Royal Delft was commissioned by William Mittendorf II, the former U. S. Ambassador to Holland, to produce a series of plates and mugs depicting famous ships. A Viking ship, painted in the rich browns characteristic of Rembrandt's masterpieces, was the first subject in this 9″ plate-and-mug series.

The 1973 edition of the Mother's Day plate depicts a mother and daughter at play; both are shown wearing the traditional costumes of the picturesque fishing village of Marken. The 1973 Father's Day plate depicts a father and son, wearing costumes from the 1600s, viewing the Zuyder Zee. Both plates are 7″ and contain a hand-painted cobalt blue underglaze.

The Royal Delft Christmas plates have been issued in two sizes (10″ and 7″) since 1915. Each series has its own sequence of scenes from Dutch life. Both are the classic cobalt blue. Random listings of prices for the older plates are included below.

All issues of Royal Delft plates are made in numbered editions of under 4,500.

Christmas Plate, 10"

[For color illustrations, see page 169.]

1. ☐ 1917	54.00		7. ☐ 1955	75.00*
2. ☐ 1918	54.00		8. ☐ 1956	75.00
3. ☐ 1920	60.00		9. ☐ 1957	62.00
4. ☐ 1921	60.00		10. ☐ 1958	65.00
5. ☐ 1922	60.00		11. ☐ 1963	90.00
6. ☐ 1929	60.00			

12. ☐ 1968	SCHREIERSTOREN		50.00
13. ☐ 1969	OLD CHURCH IN DORDRECHT		50.00
14. ☐ 1970	CATHEDRAL IN VEERE		60.00
15. ☐ 1971	CANAL SCENE IN UTRECHT		65.00
16. ☐ 1972	CHURCH OF EDAM		70.00
17. ☐ 1973	WEIGHING OFFICE AT ALKMAAR		75.00

25   26   27   28   17   24

* Prices quoted in book are approximate retail for plates in mint condition. For explanation of
A.B.P. (Average Buying Price) and Mint Condition see pages 9–11.

Christmas Plate, 7"

[*For color illustrations, see page 169.*]

18. ☐ 1964	DUTCH SCENE	62.00
19. ☐ 1968	WALMOLEN MILL, SCHIEDAM	35.00
20. ☐ 1969	MILL NEAR GORKUM	40.00
21. ☐ 1970	MILL NEAR HAARLEM	40.00
22. ☐ 1971	TOWN GATE OF ZIERKEE	45.00
23. ☐ 1972	TOWN GATE AT ELBURG	40.00
24. ☐ 1973	TOWN GATE AT AMERSFOORT	50.00

Valentine's Day Plate, 7"

25. ☐ 1973— FIRST ISSUE PIJNACKER BOUQUET		75.00

Easter Plate, 10"

26. ☐ 1973— FIRST ISSUE EASTER CROSS		75.00

Mother's Day Plate, 7"

27. ☐ 1973	MARKEN VILLAGERS	50.00

Father's Day Plate, 7"

28. ☐ 1973	LOOKING AT THE ZUYDER ZEE	50.00

Ambassador Plate, 8"

29. ☐ 1973— FIRST ISSUE VIKING SHIP		75.00

DRESDEN

(Germany)

3

5

Dresden has, for many years, been known as the place where translucent, delicate, beautiful figurines are produced. From this area of fine porcelain manufacturers now come two limited edition collector's plates. Decorated in true cobalt underglaze on the finest white baroque china, both measure 7½" in diameter. Tranquil scenes, pictured in the center, are framed by relief borders of hand-polished gold.

Issues of each edition range from 5,000–10,000 plates.

Christmas Plate, 7½"

1. ☐ 1971— FIRST ISSUE	SHEPHERD SCENE		30.00–50.00
2. ☐ 1972	NIKLAS CHURCH		15.00–20.00
3. ☐ 1973	SCHWANSTEIN CHURCH		18.00–22.00

Mother's Day Plate, 7½"

4. ☐ 1972— FIRST ISSUE	DOE AND FAWNS		32.50–40.00
5. ☐ 1973	MARE AND FOAL		15.00–20.00

FENTON ART GLASS
(U. S. A.)

2

3

Founded by Frank L. Fenton in 1905 in Martins Ferry, Ohio, the Fenton Art Glass Company is now located in Williamstown, West Virginia, just across the Ohio River from Marietta, Ohio. Frank L. Fenton, who began operations with his brother John as partner, was an experienced craftsman in the making and decorating of glass.

In 1907 iridescent, or carnival, glass was introduced by the Fenton Company, for which they soon became noted; until 1920 this remained Fenton's major product. The original formula, still in use, has been acclaimed as being extremely close in appearance to the original carnival glass. The recent introduction of a new blue marble (slag) glass has won favor among decorators and collectors.

Glass, America's first industry (beginning in 1608 in Jamestown, Va.), is the subject of Fenton's first commemorative plate, issued in 1970. It depicts the Fenton trademark—an old glassworker. The trademark glassworker is a "finisher." A blend of centuries-old skills and tools and computer-age glass technology is used to produce glass in Fenton's modern plant.

The first time that first edition commemorative and Christmas plates were made by Fenton was in 1970. In 1971 they added a Mother's Day plate. The "Christmas in America" series, consisting of Christmas plates measuring 8″ in diameter, as well as the first edition of the Mother's Day plate, are available in either a carnival or blue marble satin finish; the 1972 Mother's Day plate is also done in white satin. Early American craftsmen are portrayed in the commemorative plate, which is available only in a carnival finish. The first was the "Glass Craftsman of Jamestown," after which came the "Printer of

Cambridge, Mass." (1971), followed by the "Village Blacksmith" (1972), based on Longfellow's poem. In 1973 they issued "The Shoemaker (Cordwainer) of Salem, Mass." Fenton produced the first "Famous Lovers" Valentine's Day plate in 1972; it depicts Romeo and Juliet and is executed in bas-relief.

Production on all plates is limited to the year of issue.

Christmas Plate, 8"

1. ☐ 1970— FIRST ISSUE	LITTLE BROWN CHURCH IN THE VALE,		
	BLUE CARNIVAL GLASS	12.50–18.00
2. ☐ 1971	THE OLD BRICK CHURCH,		
	CARNIVAL OR BLUE SATIN	12.50–16.50
3. ☐ 1972	THE TWO-HORNED CHURCH,		
	CARNIVAL OR BLUE OR WHITE		
	SATIN	12.50–15.00
4. ☐ 1973	SAINT MARY'S IN THE MOUNTAINS,		
	CARNIVAL OR BLUE OR WHITE		
	SATIN	12.50–15.00

Valentine's Day Plate, 8"

5. ☐ 1972— FIRST ISSUE	ROMEO AND JULIET,		
	CARNIVAL GLASS OR BLUE SATIN	22.00

Mother's Day Plate, 8"

[For color illustrations, see page 62.]

6. ☐ 1971— FIRST ISSUE	MADONNA WITH SLEEPING CHILD,		
	CARNIVAL OR BLUE SATIN	12.50–18.00
7. ☐ 1972	MADONNA OF THE GOLDFINCH,		
	CARNIVAL GLASS, BLUE OR		
	WHITE SATIN	12.50–15.00
8. ☐ 1973	THE RAPHAEL MADONNA		
	("SMALL COWPER"),		
	CARNIVAL GLASS, BLUE OR		
	WHITE SATIN	12.50–13.50

Craftsmen Commemorative Plate, 8"

[*For color illustrations, see page 62.*]

9. ☐ 1970— FIRST ISSUE GLASSMAKER, CARNIVAL GLASS[1] 12.50–15.00
10. ☐ 1971 PRINTER, CARNIVAL GLASS 10.00–12.50
11. ☐ 1972 BLACKSMITH, CARNIVAL GLASS 10.00–12.50
12. ☐ 1973 SHOEMAKER (CORDWAINER),
CARNIVAL GLASS 10.00–12.50

[1] First issued (then recalled) in black carnival glass with the misspelling "Craftman" on back—very rare.

Anniversary Plate, 8"

13. ☐ 1972 25TH ANNIVERSARY, MILK GLASS 12.00
14. ☐ 1973 I LOVE YOU MORE TODAY THAN
YESTERDAY BUT LESS THAN
TOMORROW, MILK GLASS 10.00

9

6

11

JUAN FERRANDIZ
(Italy)

1   5

Spanish artist and humanitarian Juan Ferrandiz is known all over
the world for his dedicated work for UNESCO, his Christmas cards,
and his children's stories and illustrations. His art and love for children and nature are revealed in these lovely limited edition plates
handcrafted in carved wood and porcelain by Anri of Italy, which also
distributes a line of plates designed by Ferrandiz (see *Anri*).

Christmas Plate, 9"

1.	☐ 1972— FIRST ISSUE	FINISHING THE CRADLE, WOOD	35.00–45.00
2.	☐ 1972— FIRST ISSUE	CHRIST IN THE MANGER,	
		PORCELAIN (7½")	30.00–40.00
3.	☐ 1973	SHEPHERD AND SHEEP	40.00–50.00

Mother's Day Plate, 9"

4.	☐ 1972— FIRST ISSUE	CHILDREN PLAY HOUSE	27.50–35.00
5.	☐ 1973	MOTHER AND CHILD	40.00–50.00

Happy Birthday Plate, 8"

6.	☐ 1972— FIRST ISSUE	GIRL, DECORATION IN PINK	15.00–20.00
7.	☐ 1972— FIRST ISSUE	BOY, DECORATION IN BLUE	15.00–20.00

Wedding Day Plate, 9"

8.	☐ 1972— FIRST ISSUE	BOY AND GIRL EMBRACING	35.00–45.00
9.	☐ 1973	WEDDING SCENE	30.00–40.00

ALFONSO FONTANA/CREATIVE WORLD

(Italy)

1   3

The first issue of these unique, hand-made plates features a colorful Christmas scene with decorated Christmas trees, and three-dimensional figures with dog in the foreground.

The issues are made of Kaolin by hand craftsmen of Creative World. The edges of the plates are "crimped" in pie-plate fashion. All plates feature three-dimensional figures with colorful painted backgrounds.

Each issue of 2,000 plates is painted and numbered by hand.

Christmas Plate, 8″

1. ☐ 1972	EIGHTEENTH CENTURY COUPLE		
	WITH DOG	42.50*
2. ☐ 1973	WINTER SLEIGH RIDE	37.50

Mother's Day Plate, 8″

3. ☐ 1973	MOTHER AND CHILD	37.50

* Prices quoted in book are approximate retail for plates in mint condition. For explanation of A.B.P. (Average Buying Price) and Mint Condition see pages 9–11.

FOSTORIA
(U. S. A.)

2

One of the old-line American glass and crystal producers, Fostoria has made table items for many years. Since Fostoria is an American company, it is natural that the subjects of their limited edition crystal plates should relate to American events and the fifty states.

The series entitled "American Milestones" consists of etched and engraved scenes commemorating great events in American history. The first in this series is "The Flag." At the close of 1971, the molds for this edition were destroyed. The second issue, the "Francis Scott Key—National Anthem" plate, has an etched portrait of the composer bordered by stars and the words and music of the National Anthem. The molds for this plate were destroyed at the end of 1972. "Washington Crossing the Delaware" is the third in the series. At the close of 1973 the molds for this edition were retired. Each crystal plate comes encased in a gift box lined with black velvet.

New York, California, and Ohio are the first of a series of Fostoria crystal plates commemorating the great states that make up America. In June 1972 the molds for these editions were destroyed. Subsequent plates honor the remaining states. Each art masterpiece is handcrafted in fine crystal; the plates will inevitably appreciate in value. Acquiring the entire series will become the goal of both connoisseurs of Americana and those who prize distinguished possessions.

Editions are issued in quantities of 3,000–12,000 plates.

American Milestones Plate, 8" x 10½"

1. ☐ 1971—	FIRST ISSUE	BETSY ROSS—THE FLAG	16.00
2. ☐ 1972		FRANCIS S. KEY	13.50
3. ☐ 1973		WASHINGTON CROSSING THE DELAWARE	12.50

4. ☐ 1972	OHIO	6.50–12.50
5. ☐ 1972	NEW YORK	each
6. ☐ 1972	CALIFORNIA	
7. ☐ 1972	HAWAII	
8. ☐ 1972	TEXAS	
9. ☐ 1972	FLORIDA	
10. ☐ 1972	MASSACHUSETTS	
11. ☐ 1972	PENNSYLVANIA	
12. ☐ 1973	MICHIGAN	

4

5   6

FRANCONIA

(Germany)

    This unusual bas-relief, unglazed white china plate was issued by this prestigious porcelain company to commemorate the 1972 Olympics held in Munich.

    The famous Frauenkirche twin bulbous towers and the Olympic symbol are featured on the plate, which measures 11½″ in diameter with a ½″ bevelled border.

Commemorative Plate, 11½″

☐ 1972   XX Olympiade München   20.00

THE FRANKLIN MINT

(U. S. A.)

1

The Franklin Mint is responsible for the production of the finest sterling silver in strictly limited editions. Each sterling silver plate is individually etched and numbered, and measures 8″ in diameter. Their superb craftsmanship and the beauty of their designs are known throughout the world. The first (1970) Norman Rockwell Christmas plate, shown above, was a landmark in collectible plates. The combination of the nationally popular artist's work and the secure investment value of sterling silver helped launch the mania for sterling silver collectible plates on a large scale. Its value as a first issue, plus the additional assets of appeal and investment potential, have increased the price of this original $125 plate to over $600.

The Franklin Mint has maintained a tradition of commissioning original works by eminent artists and sculptors and reproducing them in collector plates of precious metals throughout their holiday and commemorative series. Because these vary greatly in style and artistic content, we have provided notes for each listing.

All Franklin Mint plates are serially numbered and registered.

2

3

4

5   6

Christmas Plate, 8"

[For color illustration, see cover.]

Norman Rockwell, America's best-loved artist has created pictures exclusively for this series of Franklin Mint Christmas plates. The first was issued in 1970 in an issue of 18,000. Later editions were approximately 25,000.

1. ☐ 1970— FIRST ISSUE	BRINGING HOME THE TREE	450.00–650.00*
2. ☐ 1971	UNDER THE MISTLETOE	200.00–250.00
3. ☐ 1972	THE CAROLERS	125.00–175.00
4. ☐ 1973	TRIMMING THE TREE	150.00–200.00

Easter Plate, 8"

[For color illustrations, see page 59.]

The first issue of the Franklin Mint's Easter series appeared in 1973. Eminent sculptor Evangelos Frudakis combined two precious metals in unique fashion in his design. The plate is sterling silver; the sculpted figure is 24k gold on sterling silver.

5. ☐ 1973— FIRST ISSUE	THE RESURRECTION	175.00

Mother's Day Plate, 8"

Franklin Mint's Mother's Day series first appeared in 1972. It featured a touching scene by contemporary artist Irene Spencer. The same artist created the 1973 design. Both plates are in sterling silver. Approximately 20,000 of each were issued.

6. ☐ 1972— FIRST ISSUE	MOTHER AND INFANT	125.00–175.00
7. ☐ 1973	MOTHER AND CHILD	150.00–200.00

* Prices quoted are approximate retail for plates in mint condition. Silver and gold plate prices subject to radical change due to price fluctuation of these metals. For explanation of A.B.P. (Average Buying Price) and Mint Condition see pages 9–11.

Thanksgiving Plate, 8"

Steven Dohanos, a distinguished American artist, has created wonderful original art for the first two of five annual Franklin Mint Thanksgiving plates. Each solid sterling silver plate is individually etched.

8. ☐ 1972— FIRST ISSUE   THE FIRST THANKSGIVING   125.00–175.00
9. ☐ 1973   AMERICAN WILD TURKEY   125.00–200.00

James Wyeth Annual Plate, 8"

Photographs © 1972, 1973 James Wyeth

James Wyeth will, for at least the next five years, create a plate to be issued annually. These are the first pictures exclusively created for use on silver collector plates by any member of this distinguished family of American artists. The first two are typical of James Wyeth's rural American subjects.

Approximately 20,000 of each were issued.

10. ☐ 1972— FIRST ISSUE ALONG THE BRANDYWINE   125.00–175.00
11. ☐ 1973   WINTER FOX   125.00–150.00

American West Plate, 8"

[For color illustration, see page 59.]

This is a splendid series of four collector's plates honoring vanished figures of the American West. Each plate—sculpted in bas-relief and available both in sterling silver and 22k gold—was minted from an original design made especially for this series by a distinguished American artist. The plates, capturing the feeling of the period and the region, are authentic in every detail. First in the series is "Horizons West," by Richard Baldwin, issued early in 1972; second is Gordon Phillips' "Mountain Man"; third is "Prospector," by Gus Shafer; and last is J. Weaver's "Buffalo Hunter." Each plate is serially numbered and registered in the owner's name.

Approximately 5,000 of each were issued in sterling silver. The original issue prices are shown for gold plates.

12. 1972— FIRST ISSUE	HORIZONS WEST,		
☐		STERLING SILVER	150.00
☐		22k GOLD	2200.00
13. 1972	MOUNTAIN MAN,		
☐		STERLING SILVER	150.00
☐		22k GOLD	2200.00
14. 1973	PROSPECTOR,		
☐		STERLING SILVER	150.00
☐		22k GOLD	2200.00
15. 1973	BUFFALO HUNTER,		
☐		STERLING SILVER	150.00
☐		22k GOLD	2200.00

13

14

15

R. E. Younger Bird Plate, 8"

This series of four collector's plates features original art by Richard Evans Younger, the distinguished American wildlife artist. Approximately 13,000 of each plate were issued.

16. ☐ 1971— FIRST ISSUE CARDINAL   125.00
17. ☐ 1972   BOBWHITE   125.00
18. ☐ 1973   MALLARDS   125.00
19. ☐ 1973   BALD EAGLE   125.00

National Audubon Society / J. F. Lansdowne Plate, 8"

The National Audubon Society has issued sterling silver collector's plates which are available only to the society's members and American Express card members. Each plate reproduces original art by James Fenwick Lansdowne and is individually etched and serially numbered by The Franklin Mint.

20. ☐ 1972— FIRST ISSUE GOLDFINCH   125.00
21. ☐ 1973   WOOD DUCK   125.00
22. ☐ 1973   CARDINAL   125.00
23. ☐ 1973   RUFFED GROUSE   125.00

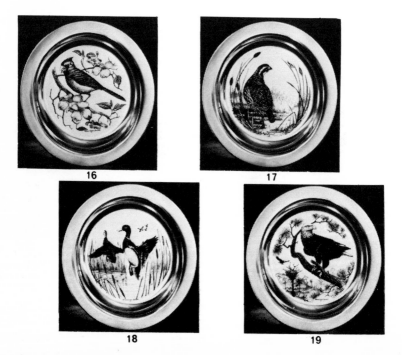

16   17

18   19

20 24 31

Presidential Plate, 8"

The White House Historical Association authorized these plates, a commemorative series created by Yves Beaugard, distinguished American artist and sculptor. They will be a complete set of gold-inlaid presidential portraits on sterling silver, to be issued monthly for a period of three years.

Approximately 10,000 of each plate were issued.

24. ☐	1972— FIRST ISSUE	GEORGE WASHINGTON	150.00
25. ☐	1973	JOHN ADAMS	150.00
26. ☐	1973	THOMAS JEFFERSON	150.00
27. ☐	1973	JAMES MADISON	150.00
28. ☐	1973	JAMES MONROE	150.00
29. ☐	1973	JOHN QUINCY ADAMS	150.00
30. ☐	1973	ANDREW JACKSON	150.00

Zodiac Plate, 8"

Gilroy Roberts, chief sculptor of The Franklin Mint, is the creator/designer of the twelve Franklin Mint Zodiac plates. He is the dean of American medallic sculptors as well as the sculptor of the Kennedy half-dollar. On his zodiac series, each sterling silver plate bears the sign's name and symbol sculpted in bas-relief. These have been issued monthly, beginning in September 1973.

31. ☐	SEPTEMBER 1973	AQUARIUS	125.00
32. ☐	OCTOBER 1973	PISCES	125.00
33. ☐	NOVEMBER 1973	ARIES	125.00
34. ☐	DECEMBER 1973	TAURUS	125.00

FRANKOMA

(U. S. A.)

The late John Frank founded this outstanding American pottery company in 1933 as a "kitchen" business and led it to its present high place. Frankoma is a tribute to his artistic ability, initiative, and faith in fine pottery; it represents the people's love for authentic American craftsmanship.

Collector's items of unusual design are produced in this factory, which uses native Oklahoma red clay. The relief of their 8½" Christmas plate really stands out; this is the result of a semitranslucent "Della Robbia" white glaze. All plates are limited editions. Special issues have also been created to commemorate the 200th anniversary of the founding of the United States.

Frankoma must be credited with the issuance of the first American annual Christmas plate in 1965. Quantities produced for each Frankoma plate range from 5,000–10,000.

Christmas Plate, 8½"

1. ☐ 1965— FIRST ISSUE	GOODWILL TOWARD MEN	175.00
2. ☐ 1966	BETHLEHEM SHEPHERDS	65.00
3. ☐ 1967	GIFTS FOR THE CHRIST CHILD	47.50
4. ☐ 1968	FLIGHT INTO EGYPT	16.00
5. ☐ 1969	LAID IN A MANGER	12.00
6. ☐ 1970	KING OF KINGS	7.50
7. ☐ 1971	NO ROOM IN THE INN	6.50
8. ☐ 1972	SEEKING THE CHRIST CHILD	5.00
9. ☐ 1973	THE ANNUNCIATION	5.00

Bicentennial Plate, 8½"

10. ☐ 1972	PROVOCATIONS	6.00
11. ☐ 1973	PATRIOTS—LEADERS	6.00

1

2

3

9

10

11

FÜRSTENBERG

(Germany)

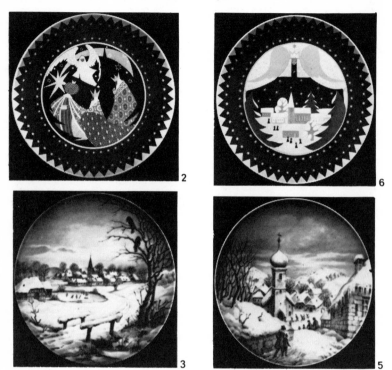

Carl I founded the Fürstenberg Porcelain factory in 1747, making it the oldest of its kind in the German Federal Republic. Fürstenberg's early wares were imitations of Meissen forms and decorations. Each item was given a blue "F" mark, which was later surmounted by a crown. The factory switched from neoclassical to more modern designs during the second quarter of the 1800s. They now create successful modern designs and produce beautiful items in baroque and empire styles, as shown by their two series of Christmas plates.

Fürstenberg's first limited edition collector's plate was issued for Easter 1971. It depicts sheep in a spring landscape. A Christmas plate was issued the same year. In 1972 the first Mother's Day plate appeared. All plates measure 7½" in diameter and are colored with cobalt blue underglaze. The only exception is the deluxe Christmas series. The plates measure 9½" in diameter; they are richly colored, bordered in cobalt blue, and are hand decorated in 18k gold. Each deluxe Christmas plate is individually signed and numbered. Quantities produced for each *regular* plate range from 2,500–4,000; quantities produced for each *deluxe* plate range from 1,000–2,000. The Olympic commemorative plate is limited to 5,000 signed and numbered pieces.

Christmas Plate, 7½" / 9½"

1. ☐ 1971— FIRST ISSUE	RABBITS (REGULAR)		15.00–20.00
2. ☐ 1971— FIRST ISSUE	THREE WISE MEN AND ANGEL (DELUXE)		45.00–90.00
3. ☐ 1972	SNOWY VILLAGE (REGULAR)		15.00
4. ☐ 1972	HOLY FAMILY AND ANGEL (DELUXE)		50.00–60.00
5. ☐ 1973	GOING TO CHURCH (REGULAR)		16.00
6. ☐ 1973	EUROPEAN VILLAGE (DELUXE)		50.00–60.00

Easter Plate, 7½"

7. ☐ 1971— FIRST ISSUE	SHEEP	65.00–85.00
8. ☐ 1972	CHICKS	15.00
9. ☐ 1973	RABBITS	16.00

Mother's Day Plate, 7½"

10. ☐ 1972— FIRST ISSUE	HUMMINGBIRDS	15.00
11. ☐ 1973	HEDGEHOGS	16.00

Commemorative Plate, 7½"

12. ☐ 1972	GYMNAST, OLYMPIADE—MÜNCHEN	25.00

12

11

10

THE GEORGE WASHINGTON MINT/ MEDALLIC ART COMPANY

(U. S. A.)

The Medallic Art Company, producers of commemorative medals for seventy-five years and manufacturer of the plates sold by the George Washington Mint, took over the operation of the latter company in 1973. They have continued to produce the George Washington Mint plates and bring out new issues which had been originally planned by the mint in its ongoing series.

An outstanding characteristic of the George Washington Mint has always been its issuance of the work of noted artists in precious metals. A series of five famous artists' representations of their mothers is the subject of the Mother's Day plate series. American artist N. C. Wyeth (father of artist Andrew Wyeth and grandfather of artist James Wyeth, who has a Franklin Mint series bearing his name) is represented in a plate series, as is the great medallist Edward Warren Sawyer. Sawyer's silver and bronze profile of Custer's Indian scout was the first of an **American Indian series being produced with the cooperation of the Bureau of Indian Affairs.** Frederick Remington is honored in the "Remington **Americana**" series **of plates, which are** double-struck in bas-relief and produced with the cooperation of the Whitney Museum of American Art. The image is struck into the base of the plate, which is shaped in the form of a gold-mining pan.

As the first in its "Great Art in Silver" series, the George Washington Mint issued an interpretation of Leonardo da Vinci's magnificent *Last Supper* in a limited edition solid silver plate. Each plate comes completely framed with a numbered and hallmarked guarantee certificate. Pablo Picasso's celebrated *Don Quixote de la Mancha* is the first subject in the "Modern Masters" series. Picasso's portrait and signature can be found stamped on the bronze base accompanying each plate; hallmark and registration are also stamped on the base.

All these plates measure 8″ in diameter, possess a mirrored border with a rolled edge, and are minted in bold relief. They are all beautifully crafted and contain truly intricate detail.

The Mother's Day, N. C. Wyeth, and Modern Masters plates are limited to 10,000 each; the Sawyer and Remington plates to 7,500 each, including sterling proof and gold issues, as noted.

Mother's Day Plate, 8"

1.	1972— FIRST ISSUE	WHISTLER'S MOTHER,	
	☐	STERLING SILVER (9,800)	150.00–200.00*
	☐	STERLING SILVER PROOF (100)	1250.00
	☐	SOLID GOLD (100)	2500.00
2.	1973	V. D. BRENNER'S *Mother and Child*,	
	☐	STERLING SILVER	175.00

N. C. Wyeth Plate, 8"

3.	1972— FIRST ISSUE	THE MIGHT OF AMERICA,	
	☐	STERLING SILVER	150.00
	☐	STERLING SILVER PROOF	1250.00
	☐	SOLID GOLD	2500.00

American Indian Plate, 8"

4.	1972— FIRST ISSUE	EDWARD D. SAWYER'S *Curley*,	
	☐	STERLING SILVER (7,300)	150.00
	☐	STERLING SILVER PROOF (100)	1250.00
	☐	SOLID GOLD (100)	2500.00
5.	☐ 1973	*Tsh-Sha-A-Nish-Is* (TWO MOONS)	
		STERLING SILVER	150.00

* *Prices quoted are approximate retail for plates in mint condition. Silver and gold plate prices subject to radical change due to price fluctuation of these metals. For explanation of A.B.P. (Average Buying Price) and Mint Condition see pages 9–11.*

1

3

4

Remington's Americana Plate, 8"

6. ☐ 1972— FIRST ISSUE THE RATTLESNAKE,

   STERLING SILVER (7,300)   175.00–250.00

   STERLING SILVER PROOF (100)   1,000.00

   SOLID GOLD (100)   2,500.00

Great Art in Silver Plate, 8"

7. ☐ 1972— FIRST ISSUE LEONARDO DA VINCI'S

   The Last Supper   125.00

Modern Masters Plate, 8"

8. 1972— FIRST ISSUE PICASSO'S *Don Quixote de la Mancha,*
   ☐   STERLING SILVER (9,800)   125.00
   ☐   STERLING SILVER PROOF (100)   1000.00
   ☐   SOLID GOLD (100)   2000.00
9. 1973   PICASSO'S *The Rites of Spring,*
   ☐   STERLING SILVER   150.00

8   9

6

GORHAM SILVER COMPANY
(U. S. A.)

The Gorham Silver Company began manufacturing silver in Providence, Rhode Island, in 1831. Their founder went from house to house with horse and wagon, showed samples of his wares, and took orders. This was a customary procedure among silversmiths of that time. The world now recognizes Gorham as the largest manufacturer of sterling silver pieces. They are the proud producers of fine quality items; the made-to-order pieces that were turned out by many of their early silver craftsmen represent some of America's most treasured heirlooms. Gorham is also the producer of a number of limited edition plates in both porcelain and silver.

An entire series of limited edition porcelain Christmas plates, based on Norman Rockwell's beloved Brown and Bigelow Calendar series, was produced by Gorham in 1971. Entitled "The Four Seasons," four of these plates are to be issued each year for sixteen years, comprising a group of sixty-four plates in all.

Two other limited edition items were made in 1971. The first is a set of fine porcelain reproductions of great paintings entitled "Gallery of the Masters." The rim of each plate is bordered by coin gold. In the second, the paintings and sketches of the actor Lionel Barrymore are reproduced in both porcelain and silver.

The home state of the buyer is inscribed on the back of Gorham's superb bicentennial plate. Developed by a Gorham artist one hundred years ago to celebrate America's centennial, memorable Revolutionary War events are illustrated in blue overglaze with 24k gold trim and lettering on fine white porcelain (the plate is also available in pewter and sterling silver).

Frederick Remington's most famous paintings of western frontier life are reproduced in a beautiful porcelain series. Also in porcelain are Gorham's cute Moppets, delightful figurines depicting children caught in amusing poses. They were featured on the Gorham Christmas and Mother's Day plates for 1973.

Norman Rockwell's Four Seasons Plate, 10½"

			Set of 4
1. ☐ 1971—	FIRST ISSUE	BOY AND DOG	120.00–200.00*
2. ☐ 1972		BOY AND GIRL	60.00–80.00
3. ☐ 1973		FOUR AGES OF LOVE	60.00–70.00

Gallery of the Masters Plate, 10½"

4. ☐ 1971—FIRST ISSUE	REMBRANDT'S	
	Man in a Gilt Helmet	50.00–60.00
5. ☐ 1972	REMBRANDT'S	
	Self-Portrait with Saskia	50.00–60.00
6. ☐ 1973	GAINSBOROUGH'S	
	The Honorable Mrs. Graham	50.00–60.00

Lionel Barrymore Plate, 8"

7. ☐ 1971— FIRST ISSUE	QUIET WATERS, PORCELAIN[1]	25.00–35.00
8. ☐ 1972	SAN PEDRO HARBOR,	
	PORCELAIN	25.00–35.00
9. ☐ 1972	LITTLE BOATYARDS,	
	STERLING SILVER[2]	100.00–150.00
10. ☐ 1973	NANTUCKET,	
	STERLING SILVER[3]	100.00–150.00

[1] limited to 15,000   [2] limited to 10,000   [3] limited to 1,000.

Bicentennial Plate, 10½"

11. 1972	THE 1776 PLATE,	
☐	PORCELAIN	25.00–35.00
☐	STERLING SILVER[1]	550.00–600.00
12. 1972	THE BURNING OF THE GASPEE,	
☐	PEWTER	30.00–40.00
☐	STERLING SILVER[2]	450.00–550.00
13. 1973	THE BOSTON TEA PARTY,	
☐	PEWTER	30.00–40.00
☐	STERLING SILVER[3]	550.00–600.00

[1] limited to 500   [2] limited to 2,500   [3] limited to 750

* Prices quoted are approximate retail for plates in mint condition. Silver and gold plate prices subject to radical change due to price fluctuation of these metals. For explanation of A.B.P. (Average Buying Price) and Mint Condition see pages 9–11.

2

8

10

5

11

95

14. ☐ 1973	A NEW YEAR ON THE CIMARRON	25.00
15. ☐ 1973	THE FLIGHT	25.00
16. ☐ 1973	THE FIGHT FOR THE WATER HOLE	25.00
17. ☐ 1973	AIDING A COMRADE	25.00

Moppets Plate, 8½"

18. ☐ 1973	MOPPETS CHRISTMAS TREE	12.50
19. ☐ 1973	MOPPETS MOTHER'S DAY PLATE	12.50

Commemorative Plate

20. ☐ 1973	25TH ANNIVERSARY OF ISRAEL	
	STERLING SILVER, LIMITED TO 200	200.00

14

18

20

GREENTREE POTTERY/HERITAGE PLATES

(U. S. A.)

11

These plates are designed by Judy Sutcliffe, an artist/potter who founded the company only five years ago. They all deal with Americana. All editions are limited to 2,000, after which the molds are destroyed. The plates, measuring 9½" in diameter, are sculpted in relief; they are handcrafted in the U.S. and glazed in a palette of complementary colors. No decals are used. Most editions are numbered 1 to 2,000. Many are sold by philanthropic organizations.

American Landmarks Plate, 9½"

1. ☐ 1970	MT. RUSHMORE, BLUE AND WHITE	10.00
2. ☐ 1971	NIAGARA FALLS	10.00

Grant Wood Plate, 9½"

3. ☐ 1971	GRANT WOOD'S STUDIO	15.00
4. ☐ 1972	GRANT WOOD'S ANTIOCH SCHOOL	15.00
5. ☐ 1973	GRANT WOOD'S STONE CITY	10.00

Historical American Cars Plate, 9½"

[For color illustrations, see page 167.]

6. ☐ 1972	1929 PACKARD	
	4-DOOR CONVERTIBLE	20.00
7. ☐ 1973	MODEL-A FORD	20.00

John F. Kennedy Plate, 9½"

8. ☐ 1973	JFK CENTER FOR THE	
	PERFORMING ARTS	15.00–20.00
9. ☐ 1973	JFK BIRTHPLACE	15.00–20.00

Mississippi River Plate, 9½"

10. ☐ 1973	TRICENTENNIAL, 1673–1973,	
	BLUE GLAZE	10.00
11. ☐ 1973	THE DELTA QUEEN, 1926–1973,	
	BLUE GLAZE	10.00

10

GUNTHER GRANGET

(Germany)

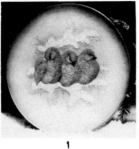

1

2

3

These beautiful, bas-relief plates are designed and sculpted by Gunther Granget, the foremost European sculptor of birds and animals. Hand-painted in natural soft tones, the plates come in two types of colors and finishes—European glaze and American matte. Reverse side imprints are also different for each type. The plates measure 12" in diameter and Granget's signature appears on the front of all plates. The 1973 Mother's Day plate issue was limited to 5,000 pieces.

Christmas Plate, 12"

1. ☐ 1972— FIRST ISSUE	SPARROWS IN WINTER,		
	AMERICAN MATTE	80.00–120.00
2. ☐ 1973	RED SQUIRREL,		
	AMERICAN MATTE	60.00–80.00

Mother's Day Plate, 12"

3. ☐ 1973	KILLDEER AND CHICK,		
	AMERICAN MATTE	75.00–100.00

99

THE HAMILTON MINT

(U. S. A.)

1

3

The National Gallery of Art granted permission to the Hamilton Mint to produce a series of three proof-finish limited edition plates entitled "Tribute to Picasso," in both sterling silver and 18k gold. Each 8″ plate was executed by the noted sculptor Alfred Brunettin, and was based upon Picasso paintings hanging in the National Gallery of Art. The first of these masterpieces is entitled *The Tragedy*, from the artist's blue period. *Le Gourmet*, painted in 1901, is the subject of the second bas-relief interpretive plate. Issued in 1972, it depicts a child tasting the contents of a bowl. The *Le Gourmet* plate was also the Hamilton Mint's first issue Christmas plate. The third in the series is *The Lovers*, based upon Pablo Picasso's famous painting of 1923. All three plates are struck in proof-finish, serially numbered, hallmarked, and packaged in custom-made gift cases. The sterling editions were limited to 4,987, and the gold to 51 pieces each.

Other sterling collector plates issued by the Hamilton Mint include "Generations of Love," also designed by Alfred Brunettin, and the St. Patrick plate, sculpted by H. Alvin Sharpe. The first, which appeared in a sterling edition limited to 1,000, was also created in gold, in an edition of only 25.

100

4

5

Tribute to Picasso Plate, 8"

1.	1972— FIRST ISSUE	THE TRAGEDY,	
	☐	STERLING	125.00–200.00*
	☐	18k GOLD	1250.00
2.	1972	LE GOURMET,	
	☐	STERLING	125.00–175.00
	☐	18k GOLD	1250.00
3.	1973	THE LOVERS,	
	☐	STERLING	125.00–160.00
	☐	18k GOLD	1250.00

Commemorative Plate

4.	1973	GENERATIONS OF LOVE, 8",	
	☐	STERLING	125.00–150.00
	☐	18k GOLD	1750.00
5.	1973	ST. PATRICK, 6",	
	☐	STERLING	75.00

* *Prices quoted are approximate retail for plates in mint condition. Silver and gold plate prices subject to radical change due to price fluctuation of these metals. For explanation of A.B.P. (Average Buying Price) and Mint Condition see pages 9–11.*

RAY HARM/SPODE

(U. S. A.)

For the Ray Harm American Songbird plates, see *Spode*.

HAVILAND & CO.

(France)

All photographs copyright © 1968, 1969, 1970, 1971,
1972, 1973 Haviland & Co., Inc.

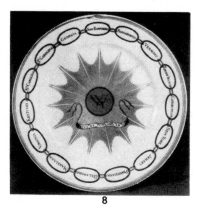

8

The firm of Haviland & Co. has always been owned and operated by an American family. When, in 1839, David Haviland left his New York-based china importing business to establish a china factory of his own in Limoges, France, little did he know that his direct descendants, now fifth generation, would be able to maintain their American citizenship and native traditions.

Haviland's limited edition Presidential Commemorative plates are tied to its history. First is the Martha Washington plate, a replica of the china presented to the First Lady by the Dutch East India Company in 1796. The second, the Lincoln plate, inaugurated the limited edition series of plates Haviland originally produced for various administrations in the White House; at the time of issue, it retailed for $100. It was followed, in 1970, by the beautiful floral plate bearing the gold crest of the United States, made for Ulysses S. Grant. The Hayes plate, third in the series, was first created in 1880 as part of the most famous set of White House china ever made. It consists of sixty-four different hand-painted pieces featuring the plants and animals of America. Plans call for the Presidential Commemorative series to be continued with reproductions of plates from the Benjamin Harrison, Andrew Johnson, and James A. Garfield administrations.

The first issue of the Haviland "Twelve Days of Christmas" plates came out in 1970 with the Partridge in a Pear Tree. Designed by Remy Hétreau, all editions are limited to 30,000; the series will end in 1981 with Twelve Drummers Drumming. The same artist (who also collaborated with Haviland on the Bicentennial series) has captured the unique quality of the French *Fête des Mères* in a charming series of seven Mother's Day plates. Each edition is limited to 10,000 individually numbered, gift-boxed plates. The Bicentennial or Independence series will consist of five issues, from 1972 to 1976, depicting the major events that led to the signing of the Declaration of Independence. It is limited to 10,000.

Christmas Plate, 8½"

1. ☐ 1970— FIRST ISSUE	PARTRIDGE IN A PEAR TREE	100.00–150.00
2. ☐ 1971	TWO TURTLE DOVES	30.00–40.00
3. ☐ 1972	THREE FRENCH HENS	30.00–35.00
4. ☐ 1973	FOUR COLLY BIRDS	30.00–32.50

Mother's Day Plate, 8¼"

5. 1973— FIRST ISSUE	#1 BREAKFAST	30.00–35.00

1   5

Bicentennial Plate, 10¼"

[For color illustrations, see page 62.]

6. ☐ 1972	1772 BURNING OF THE GASPEE	40.00–45.00
7. ☐ 1973	1773 BOSTON TEA PARTY	40.00

Presidential Commemorative Plate

8. ☐ 1968	MARTHA WASHINGTON PLATE, 8" EDITION LIMITED TO 2,500	80.00–125.00
9. ☐ 1969	LINCOLN PLATE, 10" NUMBERED EDITION LIMITED TO 2,500	130.00–180.00
10. ☐ 1970	GRANT PLATE, 10" NUMBERED EDITION LIMITED TO 3,000	130.00–150.00
11. ☐ 1971	HAYES PLATE, 10" NUMBERED EDITION LIMITED TO 2,500	130.00–150.00

7

11

HAVILAND & PARLON

(France)

1

2

This series features faithful color reproductions of French medieval tapestries from the collection of the Cloisters in New York City. The tapestries, which relate the history of the hunt for the mythical unicorn, are believed to have been made to celebrate the marriage of Louis XII to Anne of Brittany.

Each plate measures 10″ in diameter. There are approximately 10,000 in each issue. The full series will consist of six plates.

Tapestry Plate, 10″

1. ☐ 1971— FIRST ISSUE	UNICORN IN CAPTIVITY	95.00–175.00
2. ☐ 1972	START OF THE HUNT	30.00–50.00
3. ☐ 1973	UNICORN AT THE FOUNTAIN	60.00–75.00

HUMMEL-GOEBEL, SCHMID

(Germany)

All Schmid photographs copyright © 1971, 1972, 1973 Schmid Mngt.
All Goebel photographs copyright © 1971, 1972, 1973 W. Goebel (GmbH).

Berta Hummel, the artist-nun who became Sister Maria Innocentia ("M. I. Hummel") of the religious order of the Franciscans at the Convent of Siessen in Bavaria, became world famous for her inimitable sketches of children drawn at the cloister of Seissen/Wurtemberg. Her legacy to the Convent of Seissen consisted of a great many sketches as well as her personal transformation of these sketches into three-dimensional figurines.

Three series of limited edition plates now recapture the beauty of the original Hummel drawings. The first two series began with the famous "Angel in a Christmas Setting." These were issued in 1971. A Mother's Day plate formed the third series. The delicate silk-screen transfer process was used for the Christmas and Mother's Day plates. Colorful relief decorations were used for the commemorative plate.

Several different companies have manufactured Hummel plates over a period of many years. The Goebel factory of Germany (Hummelwerk) has issued a Christmas series, and Schmid Brothers of Randolph, Massachusetts, has created, produced (in a German factory), and distributed Christmas and Mother's Day plates.

These same two porcelain companies are now continuing to produce Hummel plates, and a legal dispute over the rights to Sister Hummel's drawings has resulted. Schmid claims that it should control the rights; the claim rests on a contractual agreement between Schmid and Sister Hummel's family. Meanwhile, Goebel, which had obtained a license from the cloister, tried to prevent Schmid from using the drawings. A three-judge court in Munich ruled in February 1972 that both companies should be allowed to use the Hummel pictures. Schmid plates measure 8″ in diameter; Goebel plates measure 7½″ in diameter. To distinguish between the two: Goebel designs are bas-relief with a star border. Schmid designs are screened and painted on a flat plate surface with no border.

1   2

Christmas Plate, 7½" and 8"

[For color illustrations, see page 63.]

1. ☐ 1971— FIRST ISSUE   ANGEL IN A CHRISTMAS SETTING
                          (SCHMID)   30.00–50.00*
2. ☐ 1971— FIRST ISSUE   ANGEL IN A CHRISTMAS SETTING
                          (GOEBEL)   275.00–350.00
3. ☐ 1972   SILENT NIGHT (SCHMID)   18.00–22.50
4. ☐ 1972   HEAR YE, HEAR YE (GOEBEL)   40.00–50.00
5. ☐ 1973   CHRISTMAS CRÈCHE (SCHMID)   40.00–75.00
6. ☐ 1973   GLOBE TROTTER (GOEBEL)   32.50–40.00

Mother's Day Plate, 8"

[For color illustrations, see page 63.]

7. ☐ 1972— FIRST ISSUE   PLAYING HOOKY (SCHMID)   25.00–35.00
8. ☐ 1973   THE LITTLE FISHERMAN
                          (SCHMID)   30.00–50.00

* Prices quoted in book are approximate retail for plates in mint condition. For explanation of A.B.P. (Average Buying Price) and Mint Condition see pages 9–11.

6   7

HUTSCHENREUTHER/ TIRSCHENREUTH

(Germany)

2

Fine art and fine porcelain are the two ingredients that go into this company's outstanding collector's plates. They have produced many beautiful plates, including the Granget bird plate, the Ferrandiz porcelain plate, the Hummel Christmas plate, and the Hummel Mother's Day plate. Artist John A. Ruthven, internationally acclaimed for the style and exactness of his wildlife paintings' recreation of nature, has created Hutschenreuther's Songbird series. Two full-color plates will be produced each year for a period of six years. A solid walnut case, a descriptive brochure, a certificate of registration, and Ruthven's signature accompany each plate. Each plate is individually numbered and measures 10¾" in diameter. They are distributed by the Wallace Silver Company, and the series is limited to 5,000 sets of each edition.

A limited edition 10″ porcelain plate was issued by Hutschenreuther in 1970 to commemorate the silver anniversary of the United Nations, and two famous Rembrandt paintings are also reproduced on Hutschenreuther's high-quality porcelain. Produced in nonlimited editions with diameters of 12½″, barely noticeable minor blemishes might be detected on these fine plates.

Songbirds of America Plate, 10¾″

[For color illustrations, see page 170.]

1. ☐ 1972— FIRST ISSUE	EASTERN BLUEBIRD AND GOLDFINCH	Set of 2 150.00[1]
2. ☐ 1973	MOCKINGBIRD AND ROBINS	

[1] Without box, $100.00 per set of plates.

Commemorative Plate, 10″

3. ☐ 1970	THE UNITED NATIONS' 25TH ANNIVERSARY	10.00

Rembrandt Plate, 12½″

4. ☐ 1972— FIRST ISSUE	SELF-PORTRAIT WITH SASKIA	17.50
5. ☐ 1972	MAN IN A GILT HELMET	17.50
6. ☐ 1973	THE NIGHT WATCH	17.50

4   6

IMPERIAL GLASS

(U. S. A.)

The Central Glass Works (founded in Wheeling, West Virginia, in 1860) was bought by Imperial in 1940. The molds, trademarks, etc., of the Heisey Glass Company (founded in Newark, Ohio, in 1895) were bought by Imperial in 1958. Finally, in 1960 Imperial moved all of the production facilities of the Cambridge Glass Company (founded in Cambridge, Ohio, in 1901) to its Bellaire, Ohio, factory, which was built in 1902.

At first, the Imperial Glass Corporation made low-priced glass; as time passed, their quality steadily improved, as did their design, styling, production, and merchandising; eventually they were recognized as one of America's best glass factories. Their early pieces are always in demand among collectors.

Imperial's pressed and blown glassware, introduced in 1911, is stamped or impressed with their "Nucut" trademark. In the 1913–14 period, the "iron cross" trademark was first used together with the word "Imperial." The "I" or "G" superimposed trademark was first used in 1951; the company continues to mark its wares in this way.

In 1970 Imperial issued its first limited edition collector's plate. Featured in both crystal and carnival glass, it was the first in a series of 9″ Christmas plates. The song entitled "The Twelve Days of Christmas" was chosen as its theme; each plate has a 1½″ border that features all twelve of the "gifts," with one of them enlarged in the center of the plate each year. The first in a series of 9″ crystal coin plates was issued by Imperial in 1971. The complete set of U.S. coins for 1964 (which was the last year that solid silver coins were made in the United States) is reproduced in the 1971 plate. A large reproduction of the Kennedy half-dollar is visible in the center. A 1971 set of coins is reproduced in the 1972 plate, with the Eisenhower dollar in the center.

Christmas Plate, 9"

[For color illustrations, see page 61.]

1.	1970— FIRST ISSUE	PARTRIDGE IN A PEAR TREE,	
	☐	BLUE CARNIVAL GLASS	10.00–15.00
	☐	CRYSTAL	18.50–22.50
2.	1971	TWO TURTLE DOVES,	
	☐	GREEN CARNIVAL GLASS	12.00–15.00
	☐	CRYSTAL	16.50–20.00
3.	1972	THREE FRENCH HENS,	
	☐	AMBER CARNIVAL GLASS	12.00–15.00
	☐	CRYSTAL	16.50–20.00
4.	1973	FOUR COLLY BIRDS,	
	☐	WHITE CARNIVAL GLASS	12.00–15.00
	☐	CRYSTAL	16.50–20.00

Coin Plate, 9"

5.	☐ 1971— FIRST ISSUE	JFK IN CENTER, 1964 COINS	17.50–22.50
6.	☐ 1972	IKE IN CENTER, 1971 COINS	15.00–20.00

INTERNATIONAL SILVER
COMPANY—INSILCO
(U. S. A.)

2

World-renowned for its fine tableware, the history of the International Silver Company and its predecessors is also the history of America's interest in silversmithing. Early records date back to 1808 when Ashbil Griswold, having learned his trade from the famous Danforth family, set up his pewter shop in Meriden, Connecticut. He soon expanded his business to include britannia ware. In 1852 Griswold's associates and successors, headed by Horace C. Wilcox, formed the Meriden Britannia Company—the direct forerunner of the International Silver Company.

The saga of Insilco would not be complete without a reference to the Rogers Brothers, who developed the electroplating process in 1847, thus bringing silver objects within economic reach of thousands of homes in America. The Rogers Brothers became affiliated with the Meriden Britannia Company in 1862. Since this union, "1847 Rogers Bros." has become one of the most famous international tableware trademarks.

Through the years, Insilco has developed steadily to become the largest silverware manufacturer in the world. Their unique issues of sterling silver and pewter limited edition collector's plates have been received with enthusiasm by both dealers and collectors.

For the 1976 U.S. Bicentennial, International Silver is issuing a series of six individually numbered commemorative plates of museum quality. Cast in heavyweight pewter, each 8¾" plate is rimmed with the seals of the original thirteen colonies. The design is similar to the reverse side of the Continental dollar, which was created in 1776 but was never circulated. The center of each plate bears a historic Revolutionary scene in high relief; the reverse is inscribed with the significance of the scene and the name of the sculptor.

The first, entitled "We Are One," depicts Thomas Jefferson presenting the Declaration of Independence to John Hancock, president of the Continental Congress of 1776. The second shows Paul Revere's famous ride of 1775. Every detail—from the ruffles on Paul Revere's colonial shirt to the hair on his horse's mane—is sculpted in high relief. Each of the six issues in the bicentennial series is limited to 7,500 plates. The molds will be destroyed upon completion of each edition.

International Silver's Christmas Rose plate, produced in a three-dimensional sculpted effect, captures the legend of the famous flower which unfolded in stark winter to announce the birth of the Christ child. Designed by Carl Bernhard Sundberg, the 8″ plate is crafted with a gold electroplated center design circled by solid sterling silver. The issue is limited to 2,500 plates.

Christmas Plate, 8″

1. ☐ 1972— FIRST ISSUE   CHRISTMAS ROSE, STERLING   110.00–125.00*

Bicentennial Pewter Plate, 8¾″

2. ☐ 1971— FIRST ISSUE   WE ARE ONE   50.00–75.00
3. ☐ 1972   THE MIDNIGHT RIDE
                         OF PAUL REVERE   40.00–70.00
4. ☐ 1973   WASHINGTON CROSSING
                         THE DELAWARE   30.00–50.00

3

1

* *Prices quoted are approximate retail for plates in mint condition. Silver and gold plate prices subject to radical change due to price fluctuation of these metals. For explanation of A.B.P. (Average Buying Price) and Mint Condition see pages 9–11.*

ISRAEL CREATIONS
(Israel)

This series of annual plates is produced by Naaman Ltd., the only porcelain factory in Israel. Israel Creations, Inc., is the exclusive U. S. importer and distributor of these blue and white bas-relief plates (and of all other porcelain items produced by Naaman).

The first two plates, produced in June, 1967 (shortly after the Six-Day War) depict the two holy sites in Old Jerusalem. A limited number of plates was so widely acclaimed that it was decided to continue the series with a new plate to be produced annually.

All subjects selected are of a biblical and/or an historical nature. Production of plates continues to be limited to 5,000 each; molds of previous issues are destroyed when a new plate becomes available.

Commemorative Plate, 9"

1. ☐ 1967— FIRST ISSUE	WAILING WALL		15.00–25.00
2. ☐ 1967— FIRST ISSUE	TOWER OF DAVID		10.00–15.00
3. ☐ 1968	MASADA		10.00–12.50
4. ☐ 1969	RACHEL'S TOMB		8.00–10.00
5. ☐ 1970	TIBERIAS—THE LAKE OF GALILEE		8.00–10.00
6. ☐ 1971	NAZARETH—THE NEW CHURCH OF THE ANNUNCIATION		8.00–10.00
7. ☐ 1972	BEER SHEBA		10.00–12.50
8. ☐ 1973	ACRE		12.00–15.00

GEORG JENSEN

(Denmark)

2

3

Georg Jensen, the best-known producer of fine Danish silver, entered the field of limited edition collectible plates in 1972.

The first issue of Jensen's annual Christmas plate depicts a pair of doves. This beautiful limited edition porcelain plate is 7¼" in diameter; it is colored in subtle shades of Copenhagen blue with the design in sculptured relief. The plate comes in a very attractive gift box.

The distinctive border will appear on all issues.

Christmas Plate, 7¼"

1. ☐ 1972— FIRST ISSUE DOVES		15.00–25.00
2. ☐ 1973 BOY AND DOG ON CHRISTMAS EVE		35.00–45.00

Mother's Day Plate, 7½"

3. ☐ 1973— FIRST ISSUE MOTHER AND CHILD	35.00–45.00

115

KAISER

(Germany)

The factory responsible for producing these limited edition plates in beautiful underglazes of cobalt blue and full color is noted for its quality products. Kaiser's newest creation is a series of plates commemorating great yachts. The factory considers itself the originator of the annual anniversary gift plate concept. It also produces the Berlin Design plates shown in this book.

In addition to its Christmas, Mother's Day, and anniversary series (as well as the yacht plates and other special issues in the cobalt blue), it has produced Song and Garden Birds and "Little Critter" groups. Kaiser introduced the colorful Song and Garden Birds series in 1971. The 7½" plates are produced in fine bisque porcelain, the birds, realistically hand-painted in natural tones, are depicted in woodland settings. Each issue is limited to 2,000 pieces individually numbered and certified. The six-plate "Little Critters" series features charming small animals in forest scenes. The artist for this series, Lowell Davis, is renowned for his naturalistic paintings. All plates are 8" in diameter. The Yacht plate and special issues are limited to 1,000 each. Mother's Day plates range from 7,000–8,000. The Anniversary plate, first issued in an edition of 12,000, was decreased to 7,000 in 1973.

116

Christmas Plate, 7½"

1. ☐ 1970— FIRST ISSUE	WAITING FOR SANTA	40.00–65.00*
2. ☐ 1971	SILENT NIGHT	18.00–30.00
3. ☐ 1972	WELCOME HOME	18.50–22.50
4. ☐ 1973	HOLY NIGHT	18.50–22.50

Mother's Day Plate, 7½"

5. ☐ 1971— FIRST ISSUE	MARE AND FOAL	35.00–50.00
6. ☐ 1972	FLOWERS FOR MOTHER	18.50–30.00
7. ☐ 1973	CAT AND KITTENS	18.00–20.00

Anniversary Plate, 7½"

8. ☐ 1972— FIRST ISSUE	DOVES IN THE PARK	16.50–18.50
9. ☐ 1973	HAPPY MEMORIES	18.50–22.50

Yacht Plate, 11½"

10. ☐ 1972— FIRST ISSUE	WESTWARD	50.00
11. ☐ 1972	CETONIA	50.00

Special Issues, 7½"

12. ☐ 1970	OBERAMMERGAU PLATE	25.00–30.00
13. ☐ 1970	TORONTO HORSE SHOW PLATE	32.50–40.00

Song and Garden Birds Plate, 7½"

[For color illustrations, see page 174.]

		Set of 2
14. ☐ 1971	CARDINAL AND BLUE TITMOUSE	200.00

Little Critters Plate, 8"

15. ☐ 1973	SQUIRREL, RED FOX, CHIPMUNK,	
	RABBIT, RACCOON,	Set of 6
	WHITE-FOOTED MOUSE	125.00

* Prices quoted in book are approximate retail for plates in mint condition. For explanation of A.B.P. (Average Buying Price) and Mint Condition see pages 9–11.

KING'S PORCELAIN

(Italy)

King's Porcelain is known to collectors throughout the world for its production of the original Giuseppe Cappe figurines, which are being manufactured in the King's Porcelain factory to this day.

The King's Christmas plate for 1973 was designed by Merli, a renowned horse sculptor; he has succeeded in capturing the spirit of Christmas in this high relief plate. Almost 80% of the plate's surface is sculpted and it is completely hand-painted.

King's first Mother's Day plate, entitled "The Dancing Girl," was also sculpted by Merli. The plate is completely hand-painted. The sculpture, raised about 90%, is so detailed that you can see every fingernail and hair curl. The year 1973 is embossed at the bottom of the plate; the outer rim is decorated with pure gold. "The Dancing Girl" will most certainly become a treasured collector's item.

The first plate in King's "Flowers of America" series depicts the pink carnation, widely accepted as the flower symbolizing love. Each petal is first individually executed by hand; the several flowers are then grouped together to create a most charming bouquet of pink carnations.

The Christmas and Mother's Day plates are limited to editions of 1,500. The Flowers of America plate is limited to 1,000.

3

1

2

Christmas Plate, 8½"

1. ☐ 1973— FIRST ISSUE   ADORATION OF CHRIST   140.00–160.00

Mother's Day Plate, 8"

2. ☐ 1973—FIRST ISSUE   THE DANCING GIRL   90.00–110.00

Flowers of America Plate, 8½"

3. ☐ 1973— FIRST ISSUE   THE CARNATION   80.00–90.00

SAMUEL KIRK

(U. S. A.)

"America's Oldest Silversmiths" have created several new limited edition series. A design by the eighteenth century master Giovanni Battista Tiepolo is featured in a solid sterling silver Christmas plate. Accompanying this plate is an exclusive first edition copy of *Picturesque Ideas On the Flight Into Egypt*, a beautifully illustrated and printed hard-cover history of Tiepolo's set of twenty-seven etchings (the scene on the plate was selected from among these). The Kirk Collection is presenting the book in cooperation with The Metropolitan Museum of Art. The number of copies of the book that will be produced will equal the number of Christmas plates produced.

Thanksgiving Day Ways and Means, by the American artist Winslow Homer, is the first subject of Kirk's annual Thanksgiving series. A simple portrait of a mother and child appears on the first issue Mother's Day plate. To commemorate the nation's bicentennial, the first of five plates features the earliest-known portrait of George Washington, done in 1772 by C. W. Peale; Washington is depicted as a colonel of the Alexandria Militia.

The Christmas and Thanksgiving plates are limited to 3,500 pieces each.

2

1

4

5

Christmas Plate, 8"

1. ☐ 1972— FIRST ISSUE TIEPOLO'S *The Flight into Egypt*,
STERLING SILVER 125.00–175.00*

Mother's Day Plate, 6"

2. ☐ 1972— FIRST ISSUE MOTHER AND CHILD 100.00–150.00
3. ☐ 1973 MOTHER AND CHILDREN 60.00–80.00

Thanksgiving Plate, 8"

4. ☐ 1972— FIRST ISSUE WINSLOW HOMER'S *Thanksgiving Day
Ways and Means* 125.00–175.00

American Plate, 6"

5. ☐ 1972— FIRST ISSUE WASHINGTON 75.00–85.00

* *Prices quoted are approximate retail for plates in mint condition. Silver and gold plate prices subject to radical change due to price fluctuation of these metals. For explanation of A.B.P. (Average Buying Price) and Mint Condition see pages 9–11.*

KOSTA

(Sweden)

2

The Kosta Glassworks is the oldest glass company in Sweden, having been founded in 1742 as the property of Charles XII, the "Warrior King" of Sweden. Two generals in his command founded Kosta after the defeat of the Russian army at the Battle of Narva.

Kosta crystal and glass were made in a great variety of types and styles and exported throughout the world. In 1971 Kosta produced its first annual plate. It is fashioned in clear royal blue glass and decorated with gold appliqué in modern Swedish designs.

Kosta Annual Plate, 9"

1. ☐ 1971— FIRST ISSUE	MADONNA AND CHILD	20.00–30.00
2. ☐ 1972	ST. GEORGE AND DRAGON	20.00–30.00
3. ☐ 1973	THE VIKING SHIP	30.00–40.00

LALIQUE

(France)

René Lalique (1860–1945) was one of the giants in the creative resurgence of artistic glass. His medley of precious metals, colored glass, and crystal are in museum collections. In addition, Lalique produced perfume bottles of glass and crystal for Parisian perfume manufacturers.

The Lalique glass factory, located in Alsace, France, had been producing glass and crystal since 1920, when René Lalique acquired the plant. In 1965 Lalique issued the first of a beautiful series of crystal plates, designed by Marie-Claude Lalique, granddaughter of René Lalique. The total issue for 1965 was 2,000 pieces. The plates reflect the beauty of birds, flowers, and animals. All measure 8½" in diameter, are dated, and signed "Lalique-France."

Quantities for later editions range from 2,500 to 5,000.

The original issue price for 1965 and 1966 was $25 each.

Lalique Annual Plate, 8½"

1. ☐ 1965— FIRST ISSUE	LOVEBIRDS	1,250.00–2,250.00
2. ☐ 1966	FLOWER AND LEAVES	200.00–300.00
3. ☐ 1967	FISH AND STAR	120.00–200.00
4. ☐ 1968	MOUNTAIN GOAT	100.00–150.00
5. ☐ 1969	BUTTERFLY	100.00–150.00
6. ☐ 1970	PEACOCK	75.00–125.00
7. ☐ 1971	SNOWY OWL	65.00–100.00
8. ☐ 1972	SEASHELL	65.00–90.00
9. ☐ 1973	FLEDGLING JAY	45.00–70.00

4   6   8

LENOX

(U. S. A.)

7

The Lenox China Company, founded in 1889 by Walter S. Lenox in Trenton, New Jersey, has a reputation for producing the finest American china available. Now hand-decorated plates of fine Lenox china are ushering in a unique and distinguished series of limited annual editions designed by the renowned naturalist and sculptor Edward Marshall Boehm.

Lenox has had a long and distinguished history. The White House commissioned several magnificent Lenox "Command Performance" services. The first, commissioned by President Wilson in 1917, was bordered in blue and deeply etched gold. Washington society noted that here, at last, was American china fine enough to bear the president's seal. President Roosevelt's "Command Performance" design was more personal—the gold Tudor rose and plume of the Roosevelt coat-of-arms encircles the presidential seal and forms an inner border for the blue and gold rim. President Truman's magnificent gold and green service is still being used in the White House. One of the most famous Lenox "Command Performance" services was commissioned for a special exhibit at The Metropolitan Museum of Art in New York. These $18,000-a-dozen service plates still impress connoisseurs everywhere. The first American china exhibited at the famed Ceramic Museum in Sèvres, France—the only American china to be so honored—is a Lenox coffee set.

Edward Marshall Boehm's naturalistic re-creations of birds and animals in hard-paste porcelain are valued treasures of museums,

124

heads of state, and private collectors. Amazingly lifelike detail and color are hallmarks of Boehm's art. Before his death, in 1969, Boehm created a series of designs specifically intended for reproduction on fine china. Lenox is now producing these and two other Boehm series in limited annual editions—one devoted to American birds and the other dealing with woodland wildlife. The bird series began in 1970 with the Wood Thrush, the official bird of the nation's capital. These plates, hand-crafted and lavishly decorated in 24k gold, are limited to 5,000 pieces for each issue. The first Woodland Wildlife plate was issued in a limited edition in 1973. The plate, which depicts raccoons in their natural habitat, is bordered in cobalt blue with a stylized 24k gold motif. This series is also limited to 5,000 pieces per issue.

The original issue price for 1970 and 1971 was $35 each.

Edward Marshall Boehm Bird Plate, 10½"

1. ☐ 1970— FIRST ISSUE	WOOD THRUSH		250.00–400.00
2. ☐ 1971	GOLDFINCH		150.00–225.00
3. ☐ 1972	MOUNTAIN BLUEBIRDS		75.00–125.00
4. ☐ 1973	MEADOWLARK		60.00–90.00
5. ☐ 1973	YOUNG AMERICAN BALD EAGLE		250.00–350.00
6. ☐ 1973	BIRDS OF PEACE— MUTE SWANS		350.00–550.00

Woodland Wildlife Plate, 10½"

[For color illustrations, see page 62.]

7. ☐ 1973— FIRST ISSUE	RACCOONS	75.00–125.00

| 1 | 2 | 3 |

THE LINCOLN MINT
(U. S. A.)

1

The work of great artists is used on designs for a series of items produced in sterling silver and gold by the Lincoln Mint. The first time that the Lincoln Mint issued their Great Artists plate, it created a sensation in the collectors' world. This was in 1971. In 1972 they followed this with the introduction of two new series: the Easter plate and the Mother's Day plate. These also were designed with the work of great artists serving as models. Each of these plates is individually numbered and packed in a presentation case with a certificate of authenticity; their production is strictly limited.

The first two issues of the Great Artists series and the first issue of the Easter plate were designed by a man who is truly one of the most influential artists of modern times—Salvador Dali. One plate will be issued each year until 1976, comprising a total of six plates in the Great Artists series.

Featured on the 1972 Easter plate is Dali's stylized adaptation of what the world considers his most famous painting, *Christ on the Cross*. All of the plates are executed in high relief. All come with cards which may be mailed to Salvador Dali for his personal signature.

One of the best-known oil paintings of American artist James Franzen, showing a mother collie and her pups, is reproduced for the first issue Mother's Day plate. The plates are numbered and certified, and are issued with a full-color signed lithograph. A special leatherette case comes with each plate.

The Lincoln Mint is also known for producing commemorative medals of all types.

The Easter plate is limited to an issue of 10,000.

126

Easter Plate, 8"

1. 1972— FIRST ISSUE   DALI's *Christ on the Cross*,
   ☐   STERLING SILVER   100.00–150.00*
   ☐   GOLD ON SILVER   200.00

James Franzen Mother's Day Plate, 8"

2. 1972— FIRST ISSUE   COLLIE WITH PUPS
       (WITH LITHOGRAPH),
   ☐   STERLING SILVER   75.00–125.00
   ☐   GOLD ON STERLING   150.00

Great Artists Plate, 8"

3. 1971— FIRST ISSUE   DALI's *Don Quixote on a Unicorn*,
   ☐   STERLING SILVER   100.00–200.00
4. 1972   DALI's *Dionysos et Pallas Athena*,
   ☐   STERLING SILVER   100.00–125.00
   ☐   GOLD ON STERLING   150.00
   ☐   SOLID GOLD   2,000.00
5. 1973   RAPHAEL's *Madonna della Seggiola*,
   ☐   STERLING SILVER   150.00

4   5

* *Prices quoted are approximate retail for plates in mint condition. Silver and gold plate prices subject to radical change due to price fluctuation of these metals. For explanation of A.B.P. (Average Buying Price) and Mint Condition see pages 9–11.*

LLADRO

(Spain)

1   3   6

A fine example of a new Spanish company creating beautiful and artistic porcelain plates of all types is provided by Lladro of Valencia, Spain. The Lladro brothers, Juan, Jose, and Vincente, set out to prove that Spanish porcelain was the equal of any in the world.

Although they are best known for their unique El Greco-style porcelain figurines, their first Mother's Day and Christmas plates, released in 1971, were well received by collectors and dealers. Typical of Lladro plates is the white bisque, bas-relief center with contrasting border in underglaze blue or gray.

Christmas Plate, 7¾"
---

1. ☐ 1971—	FIRST ISSUE	SINGING CAROLS	35.00–50.00
2. ☐ 1972		CAROLER	35.00–45.00
3. ☐ 1973		BOY AND GIRL,	
		CHRISTMAS TREE	47.50–52.50

Mother's Day Plate, 7¾"
---

4. ☐ 1971—	FIRST ISSUE	THE KISS OF THE CHILD	75.00–120.00
5. ☐ 1972		BIRDS AND CHICKS	30.00–40.00
6. ☐ 1973		MOTHER AND CHILDREN	35.00–45.00

LOURIOUX

(France)

This single issue is made of fine, sepia-toned porcelain; it measures 9¾″ in diameter. The makers have announced that no new issues will be produced in this series.

Châteaux of France Plate, 9¾″

☐ 1971— FIRST ISSUE   FONTAINEBLEAU   6.00–12.50

LUND & CLAUSEN

(Denmark)

2

Several interesting porcelain plates are produced by this factory. Each year a different flower is featured on the bright, colorful 7" Mother's Day plate. Well-known Danish scenes are depicted on the 7½" Christmas plate. Our intrepid Apollo explorers are depicted on the Astronaut plate.

Christmas Plate, 7½"

1. ☐ 1971— FIRST ISSUE REINDEER   13.50
2. ☐ 1972   STAVE CHURCH   13.50
3. ☐ 1973   CHRISTMAS SCENE   17.00

Mother's Day Plate, 7"

4. ☐ 1970—FIRST ISSUE	ROSE	20.00
5. ☐ 1971	FORGET-ME-NOTS	17.50
6. ☐ 1972	BLUEBELL	16.50
7. ☐ 1973	LILY OF THE VALLEY	17.00

Astronaut Plate, 7¼"

8. ☐ 1970	APOLLO 11	10.00
9. ☐ 1971	APOLLO 13	15.00

8

9

4

5

6

KAY MALLEK
(U. S. A.)

2

These unique, artistically crafted plates are fine examples of art by a group of local artists and artisans, who have applied their skills to limited edition plates. Produced in Scottsdale, Arizona, the plates feature designs by Indian, Mexican, and American artists and use as themes both Indian and Mexican customs as well as native birds. They are made with hand-applied color silk-screen stencils. The Navajo Christmas plates depict scenes of Indian family life and are true in every detail (the artists themselves are Navajos). The "Christmas in Mexico" series depicts Mexicans observing Christmas with their entire family—including pets and domesticated animals.

Kay Mallek also offers "Family Christmas," "Chinese New Year," and an Amish plate series. The "Family Christmas" series features illustrations of American birds. All plates measure 8¼" in diameter and are made of native Arizona clay; they are hand-turned on the potter's wheel.

The "Christmas in Mexico" and "Family Christmas" plate series are limited to 1,000. Navajo Christmas plates range from 1,000–2,000. The New Year and Amish plates are limited to 500.

Navajo Christmas Plate, 8¼"

[*For color illustrations, see page 167.*]

1. ☐ 1971— FIRST ISSUE INDIAN WISE MEN   45.00–85.00*
2. ☐ 1972   ON THE RESERVATION   15.00–20.00
3. ☐ 1973   INDIAN BOY AND GIRL
                        AND ANIMALS   10.00–20.00

Christmas in Mexico Plate, 8¼"

[*For color illustrations, see page 167.*]

4. ☐ 1972	MEXICAN CHRISTMAS CRÈCHE	15.00–30.00
5. ☐ 1973	THE MEXICAN HOLY FAMILY	15.00–30.00

Family Christmas Plate, 8¼"

6. ☐ 1972	THE GAMBEL QUAIL	15.00–20.00
7. ☐ 1973	THE BOB WHITE	15.00–20.00

Chinese New Year Plate, 8¼"

8. ☐ 1972	THE YEAR OF THE RAT	15.00–30.00
9. ☐ 1973	THE YEAR OF THE OX	15.00–30.00

Amish Harvest Plate, 8¼"

10. ☐ 1973	AMISH COUPLE	15.00–20.00

1

4

10

6   7

133

MARMOT

(Germany)

Appealing low relief and soft shades of blue and white underglaze are used on these 7½" limited edition porcelain plates. A deep cobalt blue in high relief is used for the commemorative plaque.

The Mother's Day plate is issued in editions of 5,000–6,000. Father's Day plates are limited to 3,000–3,500. Christmas plate editions are 2,000 each.

Christmas Plate, 7½"

1. ☐ 1970—	FIRST ISSUE	POLAR BEAR	15.00–25.00
2. ☐ 1971		BUFFALO	17.50–30.00
3. ☐ 1972		BOY AND GRANDFATHER	18.00–25.00
4. ☐ 1973		CHILDREN AND SNOWMAN	20.00–24.00

Mother's Day Plate, 7½"

5. ☐ 1972—	FIRST ISSUE	SEAL AND PUP	20.00–40.00
6. ☐ 1973		BEAR AND CUBS	40.00–60.00

Father's Day Plate, 7½"

7. ☐ 1970—	FIRST ISSUE	STAG	15.00–30.00
8. ☐ 1971		HORSE	15.00–30.00

Presidential Plate, 7½"

9. ☐ 1971—	FIRST ISSUE	GEORGE WASHINGTON	20.00–30.00
10. ☐ 1972		THOMAS JEFFERSON	25.00–32.50

5

4

METAWA
(Holland)

1

2

The "Water Gate" hallmark, a symbol of the river port of Tiel, Holland, has appeared on each piece of Metawa pewter since 1647. Apart from the characteristic hallmark and the various models, Metawa pewter can be identified by its silky finish. Pewter experts consider it a specialty unequalled to this day.

N. V. Metawa introduced its first Christmas plate in 1972 in a limited edition of 3,000. The typically Dutch scene shows Hans Brinker skating along the flooded canals. The second Metawa Christmas plate, issued in 1973, is far more elaborate than the earlier one. Executed in bas-relief, the plate depicts a 19th century scene of a couple riding in a one-horse open sleigh through a typically medieval Dutch town. All plates in the series are numbered separately and marked with the "Water Gate" symbol of quality. Only 1,500 of the 1973 plates were issued.

Christmas Plate

1. ☐ 1972— FIRST ISSUE	ICE SKATERS—HANS BRINKER	36.00
2. ☐ 1973	ONE-HORSE SLEIGH	30.00

METLOX
(U. S. A.)

1

2

3

Songs of Christmas are commemorated on this white pottery, finished and carved in the Della Robbia tradition. The colorful plates, made by the producers of Vernonware, are hand-painted.

Christmas Plate

1. ☐ 1971— FIRST ISSUE	TWELVE DAYS OF CHRISTMAS	35.00–45.00
2. ☐ 1972	JINGLE BELLS	17.50–25.00
3. ☐ 1973	THE FIRST NOËL	25.00–35.00

MOSER

(Czechoslovakia)

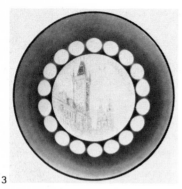

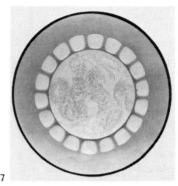

3   7

Each plate is signed and numbered, and is copper-wheel engraved on delicately colored, hand-cut fine crystal. This company has, for centuries, produced glass of tremendous beauty; these items are a fine example of their craft.

Mother's Day plates range in issue quantity from 350–750.

Christmas Plate, 7¾"

1. ☐ 1970— FIRST ISSUE	HRADCANY CASTLE, LAVENDER		300.00–600.00*
2. ☐ 1971	KARLSTEIN CASTLE, PALE GREEN		75.00–125.00
3. ☐ 1972	OLD TOWN HALL		85.00–135.00
4. ☐ 1973	KARLOVY VARY CASTLE		95.00–145.00

Mother's Day Plate, 7¾"

5. ☐ 1971— FIRST ISSUE	PEACOCKS, PALE GREEN	130.00–200.00
6. ☐ 1972	BUTTERFLIES, COBALT BLUE	85.00–140.00
7. ☐ 1973	SQUIRRELS	95.00–120.00

* Prices quoted in book are approximate retail for plates in mint condition. For explanation of A.B.P. (Average Buying Price) and Mint Condition see pages 9–11.

MUELLER, WUERFUL/SCHMID

(Germany)

1

4

After making beer steins for a considerable period of time, this Bavarian company began, in 1971, to make beautiful limited edition collector's items. A Christmas stein with a matching plate was issued both in 1971 and 1972. All plates are designed by Schmid Brothers and are distributed under their name.

Christmas Plate, 9½"

1. ☐ 1971— FIRST ISSUE	CHRISTMAS IN THE TYROL		17.50–22.50
2. ☐ 1972	MEDIEVAL CHRISTMAS		
	MESSENGER		15.00–17.50
3. ☐ 1973	BRINGING HOME THE TREE		20.00–24.00

Father's Day Plate, 9½"

4. ☐ 1973— FIRST ISSUE	SON, FATHER, GRANDFATHER		17.50–22.50

139

NIDAROS

(Norway)

1

3

A hand-etched design depicting a different landmark of "Historic Norway" is featured each year on this limited edition plate. It is an aluminum plate enameled in blue, red, or green "Norskolors."

Christmas Plate, 7¼"

1. ☐ 1970— FIRST ISSUE	NIDAROS CATHEDRAL		12.50–15.00
2. ☐ 1971	STAVE CHURCH		13.00–16.00
3. ☐ 1972	GOKSTAD VIKING SHIP		13.00–16.00
4. ☐ 1973	AKERSHUS CASTLE		15.00–17.50

ORREFORS

(Sweden)

4 3 6

The fine crystal collector's pieces made by this renowned Swedish crystal company have been sold throughout the world to the wealthy. With the introduction of limited edition plates, Orrefors' craftsmanship was made available to the general public. World-famous churches of all denominations are portrayed in one series of beautiful limited edition plates; they are handmade in exquisite clear crystal decorated with 24k gold. The intricate lines of the drawings are etched into the surface of the glass and are then filled with gold. The Mother's Day series, of which only 1,500 of the 1972 and 1973 editions were issued for U.S. distribution, is made of deep blue crystal, and is also decorated in 24k gold.

Mother's Day Plate, 8"

1. ☐ 1971— FIRST ISSUE	FLOWERS FOR MOTHER	65.00–85.00
2. ☐ 1972	MOTHER WITH CHILDREN	45.00–55.00
3. ☐ 1973	MOTHER AND BABY	50.00–60.00

Cathedral Plate, 10"

4. ☐ 1970— FIRST ISSUE	NOTRE DAME CATHEDRAL	60.00–80.00
5. ☐ 1971	WESTMINSTER ABBEY	35.00–65.00
6. ☐ 1972	BASILICA DI SAN MARCO	45.00–65.00
7. ☐ 1973	COLOGNE CATHEDRAL	40.00–60.00

PEANUTS

(Japan)

1   3

For the Peanuts series, Charles Schulz has created original artwork exclusively for Schmid Brothers, who manufacture these plates and distribute them in the U.S. The plates are made of fine porcelain. The series began in 1972 with the first edition of the Peanuts Mother's Day plate, "Linus with a Rose for Mother." A total of 15,000 plates were made before the mold was destroyed. (All molds are destroyed prior to the date specified on the plate.)

The first Peanuts Christmas plate also appeared in 1972 in an edition of 20,000. It showed Snoopy in a sleigh drawn by his friend Woodstock. The 1973 Mother's Day plate, in an edition of 8,000, shows Snoopy looking questioningly at Woodstock, who is holding a sign saying "Mom?" The two characters have been bosom buddies for so long that the question is quite appropriate. The 1973 Christmas plate depicts Snoopy reclining on his doghouse, surrounded by stockings, and eagerly awaiting Santa Claus.

Christmas Plate, 8"

[*For color illustrations, see page 174.*]

1. ☐	1972— FIRST ISSUE	WOODSTOCK PULLING SNOOPY'S SLEIGH	12.00
2. ☐	1973	WOODSTOCK WAITING FOR SANTA	10.00

Mother's Day Plate, 8"

3. ☐	1972— FIRST ISSUE	LINUS WITH A ROSE FOR MOTHER	12.00
4. ☐	1973	WOODSTOCK WITH "MOM" SIGN	10.00

PICKARD

(U. S. A.)

2

Pickard china is recognized as one of the truly fine chinas. The light ivory body is translucent and fully vitrified. The glaze is perhaps the hardest produced in domestic fine china, and all decorations are fired on glazed ware. They have been issuing collector plates since 1970.

Pickard was founded in 1893 and is now in its third generation of Pickard family ownership. Located in Antioch, Illinois, about fifty miles northwest of Chicago, the company employs eighty-five people, including some skilled decorators who are graduates of a five-year school in Selb, Germany.

In 1970 Pickard entered into a joint merchandising effort with Fostoria Glass Company, thus establishing an affiliation in the fields of sales, advertising, and design (although both firms are independently owned and operated).

The collector plates include a series of birds, reproductions of original paintings by James Lockhart of Lake Forest, Illinois, and a series of presidential portraits. On the bird series, the forest green

143

border is overlaid with a gold scroll, with gold embossing at inner and outer edges of the rim. Each bird plate is individually numbered and limited to 2,000. The eight bird plates (a complete set) were introduced annually in pairs. The Presidential series varies in detail and edition size.

Lockhart Birds Plate, 10⅝"

[For color illustrations, see page 170.]

1. ☐ 1970— FIRST ISSUE	GAME BIRDS: RUFFED GROUSE	Set of 2	
	AND WOODCOCK	300.00–400.00*	
2. ☐ 1971	WATERFOWL: MALLARD AND	Set of 2	
	GREEN-WINGED TEAL	175.00–250.00	
3. ☐ 1972	SONGBIRDS: MOCKINGBIRD	Set of 2	
	AND CARDINAL	175.00–250.00	
4. ☐ 1973— FINAL ISSUE	GAME BIRDS: WILD TURKEY AND	Set of 2	
	RING-NECKED PHEASANT	175.00–250.00	

Presidential Plate, 10⅝"

[For color illustrations, see page 170.]

5. ☐ 1971   HARRY S. TRUMAN PLATE.
         GREEN BORDER, GOLD SCROLL
         AND TRIM, SEPIA IMAGE.
         LIMITED EDITION OF 3,000   40.00

6. ☐ 1973   ABRAHAM LINCOLN PLATE.
         COBALT BLUE BORDER, GOLD SCROLL
         AND TRIM, CHARCOAL GRAY IMAGE.
         LIMITED EDITION OF 5,000   40.00

* Prices quoted in book are approximate retail for plates in mint condition. For explanation of A.B.P. (Average Buying Price) and Mint Condition see pages 9–11.

GILBERT POILLERAT/
CRISTAL D'ALBRET

(France)

The art of making sulphide paperweights was revived nearly twenty years ago by this well-known sculptor and designer. He has now created two limited edition plates containing 24% pure lead crystal. Made at France's prestigious Cristal d'Albret glass factory, each plate is individually numbered and artistically sculpted. These beautiful creations are distributed by Paul Jokelson.

In addition to the crystal plates, the fine enameling artists of Limoges and Poillerat have created a lustrous metal plate of high-quality copper and enamels. The bright enamel colors decorating the Christmas plates are circled in brass.

Christmas Plate, 11"

1. ☐ 1972—	FIRST ISSUE	BIRD OF PEACE (*Pax*)	125.00–200.00

Christmas Enamel Plate, 11"

[*For color illustrations, see page 61 .*]

2. ☐ 1972—	FIRST ISSUE	THE THREE KINGS	375.00
3. ☐ 1973		ROSE DE NOËL (CHRISTMAS ROSE)	375.00

Four Seasons Crystal Plate, 9"

4. ☐ 1972—	FIRST ISSUE	SUMMER	150.00–225.00
5. ☐ 1973		SPRING	100.00–150.00
6. ☐ 1973		AUTUMN	85.00–115.00

POOLE POTTERY, LTD.

(England)

1

The Medieval Calendar plates were designed by Tony Morris and represent several years' work with special techniques by the Craft Section of Poole Pottery. Each plate, crafted by hand in clay, is sprayed with a red coat of clay to enrich the final surface. The first firing fuses the clays together; the hard "biscuit" plate is then decorated by artists, who initial the reverse. The stained glass effect is produced by applying the black outline with a resist medium; the glaze is floated on with a brush. Mottled colors are obtained by painting glaze over glaze. A final gloss firing results in the finished piece—a work of old-world beauty produced by a modern age. Two plates are issued each year in limited editions of 1,000; each is numbered and comes with a signed certificate in a presentation box. Only 500 are available for U. S. distribution.

Medieval Calendar Plate, 12"

[*For color illustrations, see page 172.*]

1. ☐ 1972— FIRST ISSUE	JANUARY—DRINKING WINE BY THE FIRE	85.00–125.00*
	FEBRUARY—CHOPPING WOOD	85.00–125.00
2. ☐ 1973	MARCH—DIGGING IN THE FIELD	85.00–125.00
	APRIL—CARRYING THE BRANCH	85.00–125.00

PORCELAIN DE PARIS

(France)

The prestigious French atelier Porcelain de Paris, makers of fine porcelain for over 200 years, has produced the "Eight Immortals" plates, a handsome set of eight hand-enameled plates. Ancient Chinese temple jars were the inspiration for this magnificent series. Each depicts, in brilliant colors, one of the eight Chinese apostles of the great Prophet Lao Tse.

Only 300 sets of the eight plates are being made. They will be issued in two groups, each group consisting of four plates. The first group was issued in 1973; the second is to be issued in 1974. The plates were produced for the Ellis-Barker Silver Company, a subsidiary of Towle Silversmiths.

The Eight Immortals Plate, 9¾"

[*For color illustrations, see page 172.*]

☐ 1973	HO SIEN KOO, LU TUNG PIN,	
	HAN CHING-LI, CHANG-	Set of 4
	KWO-LAO	175.00

PORSGRUND

(Norway)

2

6

The Porsgrund Porselaensfabrik Company of Norway has been responsible, since 1889, for the production of many excellent limited edition items. After the enthusiastic response that greeted their 1968 Christmas plate, they were encouraged to create other items, including the deluxe variation of their Christmas plates. On the Castle plate, the castle design is done in finely detailed brown. All of the plates feature pure shades of underglaze blue on white porcelain.

In 1909 Porsgrund issued a very small edition of flower-design Christmas plates. They are very rare and are valued in excess of $600 each.

Christmas Plate, 7"

[For color illustrations, see page 64.]

1. ☐ 1968—	FIRST ISSUE	CHURCH SCENE	150.00–200.00
2. ☐ 1969		THREE KINGS	15.00–30.00
3. ☐ 1970		ROAD TO BETHLEHEM	10.00–20.00
4. ☐ 1971		A CHILD IS BORN	12.00–15.00
5. ☐ 1972		HARK THE HERALD ANGELS SING	13.00–16.00
6. ☐ 1973		PROMISE OF THE SAVIOR	15.00–20.00

Deluxe Christmas Plate, 10"

[*For color illustrations, see page 64.*]

7. ☐	1970— FIRST ISSUE	ROAD TO BETHLEHEM	60.00–100.00
8. ☐	1971	A CHILD IS BORN	40.00–60.00
9. ☐	1972	HARK THE HERALD ANGELS SING	40.00–60.00
10. ☐	1973	PROMISE OF THE SAVIOR	40.00–60.00

Easter Plate, 7"

11. ☐	1972— FIRST ISSUE	DUCKS	12.00–24.00

Mother's Day Plate, 5"

[*For color illustrations, see page 64.*]

12. ☐	1970— FIRST ISSUE	MARE AND FOAL	15.00–25.00
13. ☐	1971	GOOSE AND GOSLINGS	7.50–15.00
14. ☐	1972	DOE AND FAWN	7.50–15.00
15. ☐	1973	CAT AND KITTENS	7.50–15.00

10

21

14   **18**

Father's Day Plate, 5"

[For color illustrations, see page 64.]

16. ☐ 1971—	FIRST ISSUE	FATHER AND SON FISHING	8.50–13.50
17. ☐ 1972		COOKOUT	7.50–12.50
18. ☐ 1973		FATHER AND SON SLEDDING	12.50–14.50

Castle Plate, 7"

19. ☐ 1970—	FIRST ISSUE	HAMLET'S CASTLE	6.00–9.00
20. ☐ 1971		ROSENBORG CASTLE	6.00–9.00

Commemorative Plate, 7"

21. ☐ 1972	LEIF ERIKSON	11.00

Jubilee (Five-Year) Plate, 11"

22. ☐ 1970—	FIRST ISSUE	FEMBØRINGER	15.00–22.00

Zodiac Plate, 7"

23. ☐ 1972	12 SIGNS	6.00 Each

PUIFORCAT
(France)

Designed by the world-famous firm of Puiforcat in Paris, these *Carte à Jouer* plates were created and painted by the master surrealist artist Salvador Dali. They were produced in Limoges, France, in a limited edition of 2,000 numbered sets. Each plate bears the Dali signature imprint.

Puiforcat has also produced fine silver since 1820. In connection with La Monnaie De Paris, the world's foremost government mint, they have issued a sterling silver plate, "L'Exodus," commemorating the twenty-fifth anniversary of the State of Israel. Designed by William Schiffer, the plate depicts a boat-shaped menorah crowned by an abstract Star of David. The edition of this plate is limited to 2,000 pieces. Each plate is individually numbered.

Playing Card Plate, 9½"

[*For color illustrations, see page 169.*]

1. ☐ 1973	Royal Flush and a Joker	Set of 5	
		250.00–300.00	

Commemorative Plate (Silver), 8½"

2. ☐ 1973	L'Exodus (25th Anniversary of the State of Israel)	200.00*

* Prices quoted are approximate retail for plates in mint condition. Silver and gold plate prices subject to radical change due to price fluctuation of these metals. For explanation of A.B.P. (Average Buying Price) and Mint Condition see pages 9–11.

REED & BARTON
(U. S. A.)

One of America's oldest and finest silversmiths, Reed & Barton of Taunton, Massachusetts, has created a unique series of plates by using the ancient technique of damascene—combining silver with copper and bronze inlays to achieve a three-dimensional, multicolored effect in warm, glowing hues.

All the series produced by Reed & Barton reflect this technique. The Audubon plates, limited to 5,000 for each issue, are reproduced from drawings of North American birds by the famous naturalist. Although most of the Christmas plates illustrate religious carols, the first issue, "A Partridge in a Pear Tree," is based on the traditional folk carol; it was limited to 2,500 pieces. Subsequent Christmas plate issues have been limited to 7,500 each.

The "Kentucky Derby" series (1,000 for each issue) expresses aspects of this famous annual race. Reed & Barton has also issued a number of special commemoratives, in damascene, on Americana subjects in editions of 1,000–1,500 each; they range in price from $75–$100. In many cases, they have been distributed by other firms.

Christmas Plate, 11"

[For color illustrations, see page 60.]

1. ☐ 1970—	FIRST ISSUE	PARTRIDGE IN A PEAR TREE	85.00–125.00*
2. ☐ 1971		WE THREE KINGS	40.00–65.00
3. ☐ 1972		HARK THE HERALD ANGELS SING	40.00–65.00
4. ☐ 1973		ADORATION OF THE KINGS	40.00–65.00

Audubon Plate, 11"

5. ☐ 1970—	FIRST ISSUE	PINE SISKIN	80.00–100.00
6. ☐ 1971		RED-SHOULDERED HAWK	40.00–65.00
7. ☐ 1972		STILT SANDPIPER	40.00–65.00
8. ☐ 1973		CARDINAL	40.00–65.00

* *Prices quoted are approximate retail for plates in mint condition. Silver and gold plate prices subject to radical change due to price fluctuation of these metals. For explanation of A.B.P. (Average Buying Price) and Mint Condition see pages 9–11.*

9. ☐ 1972— FIRST ISSUE KENTUCKY DERBY   85.00
10. ☐ 1973   RIVA RIDGE   75.00

2

4

5

6

7

8

RORSTRAND

(Sweden)

6

Located in Scandinavia, this company (founded in 1726) is the oldest porcelain factory in Sweden, and the second oldest in Europe. They produced Christmas plates from 1904 to 1925, but discontinued making them until 1968. They began their new series with square-shaped, feldspar china colored in underglaze Scandia blue. Their Mother's and Father's Day plates are round and have the same coloring as the Christmas plates. Folk traditions and famous stories of Sweden are portrayed on all of these limited edition plates.

Christmas Plate, 7½"

1. ☐ 1968— FIRST ISSUE	BRINGING HOME THE TREE		100.00–150.00
2. ☐ 1969	FISHERMAN SAILING HOME		15.00–22.50
3. ☐ 1970	NILS WITH HIS GEESE		12.00–18.50
4. ☐ 1971	NILS IN LAPLAND		10.00–15.00
5. ☐ 1972	DALECARLIAN FIDDLER		10.00–15.50
6. ☐ 1973	FARM IN SMALAND		12.00–18.00

Mother's Day Plate, 8"

7. ☐ 1971— FIRST ISSUE	MOTHER AND CHILD	15.00–20.00
8. ☐ 1972	SHELLING PEAS	15.00–20.00
9. ☐ 1973	OLD FASHIONED PICNIC	16.00–20.00

Father's Day Plate, 8"

10. ☐ 1971— FIRST ISSUE	FATHER AND CHILD	15.00–20.00
11. ☐ 1972	A MEAL AT HOME	15.00–25.00
12. ☐ 1973	THE REAPERS	16.00–20.00

9

12

ROSENTHAL

(Germany)

10

Rosenthal has been making porcelain Christmas plates since 1910. The firm has won worldwide renown for producing superior-quality china. Its plates depict winter and Christmas scenes embossed in deep, clear shades of blue-green, brown, gold, white, etc. In 1971 Rosenthal stopped producing back issues; this has increased the value of these items.

The signature of the Danish artist Bjørn Winblad appears on a special line of porcelain Christmas plates. Each plate bears his highly original, intricate modern designs.

Christmas Plate, 8½"

1. ☐	1910—1967	GERMAN CHRISTMAS SCENES	75.00 Each
2. ☐	1968	CHRISTMAS IN BREMEN	50.00–75.00
3. ☐	1969	ROTHENBURG ON THE TAUBER	50.00–75.00
4. ☐	1970	COLOGNE ON THE RHINE	50.00–75.00
5. ☐	1971	GARMISCH-PARTENKIRCHEN	40.00–65.00
6. ☐	1972	MIDNIGHT MASS	40.00–65.00
7. ☐	1973	THE GATES OF LÜBECK	60.00–80.00

Bjørn Winblad Christmas Plate, 11½"

[For color illustrations, see page 61.]

8. ☐	1971— FIRST ISSUE	MARY AND CHILD	175.00–200.00
9. ☐	1972	HOLY KING CASPAR	80.00–120.00
10. ☐	1973	MOTHER AND CHILD	80.00–120.00

ROYAL BAYREUTH

(Germany)

Royal Bayreuth, the oldest privately managed porcelain factory in Bavaria, is a subsidiary of Royal Tettau (also listed in this book). It has produced fine porcelain for over 178 years. Old pieces of porcelain bearing the Royal Bayreuth hallmark are among the most sought-after objects, bringing extremely high prices for even common items.

Before World War I, Royal Bayreuth was inspired by the books of E. O. Graver to create numerous pieces depicting the busy Sunbonnet Babies. A single plate from the immensely popular original set of seven plates now brings well over $125! Royal Bayreuth is again producing the seven Sunbonnet Babies plates, faithfully reproducing each color as it appeared in the original collection. The plates show activities for each day of the week: Sunday, fishing; Monday, washing; Tuesday, ironing; Wednesday, mending; Thursday, scrubbing; Friday, sweeping; Saturday, baking. The notice on the back of each plate clearly states that this is a limited edition for that particular year (to protect the value of the premium-priced originals). There will be 15,000 serially numbered plates in all.

Christmas scenes typical of quaint Bavarian villages are depicted on the Royal Bayreuth Christmas plates. The Christmas edition is limited to 5,000 serially numbered pieces. A contemporary painting appears on the 1973 first issue of Royal Bayreuth's Mother's Day plate.

Christmas Plate, 8"

[For color illustrations, see page 63.]

1. ☐ 1972— FIRST ISSUE   CHRISTMAS SCENE WITH COACH
                          AND HORSES   40.00–80.00*
2. ☐ 1973   BAVARIAN VILLAGE WITH
                          BRIDGE   18.50–22.00

Mother's Day Plate, 7½"

3. ☐ 1973— FIRST ISSUE   MOTHER'S CONSOLATION   17.50–20.00

Sunbonnet Babies Plate, 7"

[For color illustrations, see page 63.]

4. ☐ 1973/4   SUNDAY—FISHING, MONDAY—   Set of 7
                          WASHING, TUESDAY—IRONING,   120.00
                          WEDNESDAY—MENDING,
                          THURSDAY—SCRUBBING, FRIDAY—
                          SWEEPING, SATURDAY—BAKING

2

3

4

ROYAL COPENHAGEN

(Denmark)

The Royal Copenhagen porcelain factory, the oldest existing factory of industrial art in Denmark, was established in 1775. Its unmistakable trademark, three blue wavy lines, symbolizes the three Danish waterways—the Sound, the Great Belt, and the Little Belt. The Royal Crown indicates that, at one time, the majority of shares were owned by the Royal Family. During the past 200 years, countless pieces of porcelain, stoneware, and faience bearing this trademark have been collected throughout the world.

Since 1903 Royal Copenhagen Christmas plates have featured different religious motifs and typical Danish winter scenes. They are manufactured by a special technique. A skilled craftsman carves the picture in a plaster mold, thus interpreting the artist's design. This hand-carved mold is the master for subsequent molds. Painters then decorate each plate by hand with the blue underglaze color. The plate is glazed and fired to preserve the painting underneath. Each plate is made for one year only; when the limited production is completed, the molds are destroyed. Normally, the plates are sold out within a short time and can subsequently be acquired only as collector's items. The blue Christmas plates have become treasured items; each year thousands of enthusiastic art collectors await their annual appearance.

Royal Copenhagen plates are subject to the most exacting standards. Those plates that fall below an acceptable level are marked seconds by placing one stroke through the "wave" hallmark, and thirds by placing two strokes through the hallmark. Complete sets of Royal Copenhagen Christmas plates (1908–1973) in mint condition have retailed for as high as $7,500–9,500.

Other series issued by Royal Copenhagen include a Mother's Day sequence, which began in 1971 with an edition of 20,000 (now up to about 40,000), and a Danish cathedral series in cobalt blue porcelain, which uses original paintings by Kai Lange. Since the 1880s, the company has also produced more than 300 commemoratives and special issues, many of which celebrate events in Danish history and scenes of Danish life.

Christmas Plate, 7"

[For color illustrations, see page 64.]

All the Royal Copenhagen Christmas plates are pictured. The listed price for each plate is approximate retail for plates in mint condition. The increase in these editions over the years is a testament to their popularity. In 1940–46, 4,000 each year; 30,000 from 1947–51; 60,000 from 1952–58; 100,000 from 1959–67; 200,000 since then.

| ☐ 1908 | 1275.00 | ☐ 1909 | 120.00 | ☐ 1910 | 110.00 |
| ☐ 1911 | 135.00 | ☐ 1912 | 135.00 | ☐ 1913 | 125.00 |

☐ 1914   115.00   ☐ 1915   105.00   ☐ 1916   75.00

☐ 1917   75.00   ☐ 1918   75.00   ☐ 1919   75.00

☐ 1920   66.00   ☐ 1921   60.00   ☐ 1922   60.00

☐ 1923   60.00   ☐ 1924   75.00

☐ 1925   66.00   ☐ 1926   66.00   ☐ 1927   100.00

☐ 1928   70.00   ☐ 1929   70.00

☐ 1930   69.00   ☐ 1931   74.00   ☐ 1932   72.00

☐ 1933   90.00   ☐ 1934   98.00

☐ 1935   112.00   ☐ 1936   118.00

☐ 1937   130.00   ☐ 1938   250.00   ☐ 1939   250.00

☐ 1940   450.00   ☐ 1941   450.00

☐ 1942   450.00   ☐ 1943   540.00   ☐ 1944   150.00

☐ 1945   375.00   ☐ 1946   135.00

☐ 1947   222.00   ☐ 1948   110.00

☐ 1949   140.00   ☐ 1950   135.00   ☐ 1951   260.00

☐ 1952   85.00   ☐ 1953   85.00

☐ 1954   125.00   ☐ 1955   225.00   ☐ 1956   126.00

☐ 1957   85.00   ☐ 1958   102.00

☐ 1959   124.00   ☐ 1960   120.00

☐ 1961   120.00   ☐ 1962   165.00   ☐ 1963   51.00

☐ 1964   57.00   ☐ 1965   54.00

☐ 1966   50.00   ☐ 1967   40.00   ☐ 1968   30.00

165

☐ 1969   24.00   ☐ 1970   22.00

☐ 1971   21.00   ☐ 1972   22.50   ☐ 1973   24.00

Mother's Day Plate, 6"

[For color illustrations, see page 64.]

1. ☐ 1971— FIRST ISSUE   MOTHER AND CHILD   75.00–125.00
2. ☐ 1972   MOTHER AND CHILDREN   16.00–20.00
3. ☐ 1973   MOTHER AND CHILD   18.00–22.50

1   **2**   **3**

Commemorative and Special Issue Plate

4. ☐ 1967	VIRGIN ISLANDS PLATE, 7¼"	20.00–30.00
5. ☐ 1969	DANNEBORG FLAG PLATE, 8"	20.00–30.00
6. ☐ 1969	MOON LANDING PLATE, 7¼"	15.00–20.00
7. ☐ 1970	REUNION PLATE (1920–1970), 8"	18.00–24.00
8. ☐ 1972	MUNICH OLYMPIAD PLATE, 8"	22.50–28.00
9. ☐ 1972	KING FREDERIK 25TH ANNIVERSARY PLATE, 7"	22.50–28.00
10. ☐ 1969	SUMMER MERMAID SPECIAL ISSUE PLATE, 8"	28.00–34.00
11. ☐ 1970	STATUE OF LIBERTY PLATE, 8"	22.50–28.00

4   **5**   **6**

(ROYAL COPENHAGEN LISTINGS CONTINUED ON PAGE 175.)

On the Reservation, left, and *Mexican Christmas Creche*, right
Kay Mallek, 1972

Model-A Ford
Greentree-Heritage, 1973

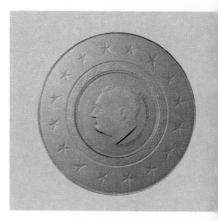

Portrait of FDR
Wheaton/Nuline, 1971

Generation of Peace
Count Agazzi, 1973

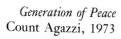

Vermeer's *The Geographer* (1973), left, and below, *Christmas in Rothenburg* (1971) Berlin Design

Travel on the Moon, left, and *Oh Tannenbaum*, right Seven Seas Traders, 1971

Weighing Office at Alkmaar (10″) and *Town Gate at Amersfoort* (7″) Royal Delft, 1973

Dali's *Cartes à Jouer*
Puiforcat, 1973

Eastern Bluebird and Goldfinch
Hutschenreuther, 1972

Above, *Portrait of Harry S. Truman*
(1971), and right, *Songbirds: Cardinal*
(1972) Pickard

Stag
Veneto Flair, 1971

U.S. Capitol Building (1969) above,
and *Liberty Bell* (1973)
America the Beautiful

Fisherman and *Old Lady Reading*
Boch Frères Delft, 1971

Two of *The Eight Immortals*
Porcelain de Paris, 1973

March and *April*
Poole Pottery, 1973

Russell's *A Doubtful Visitor*
Antique Trader, 1971

Passover Plate
Spode, 1972

Mother Sewing a Quilt
Stumar, 1973

Liberty Bell
Taylor-Smith & Taylor, 1973

Cardinal and Blue Titmouse
Kaiser, 1971

Madonna and Child
Veneto Flair, 1973

Woodstock Waiting for Santa
Peanuts, 1973

7   8   9

10   12

16   20   21

Danish Cathedral Plate, 7½"

12. ☐ 1970	AALBORG		19.50–24.00
13. ☐ 1970	KALUNBORG		19.50–24.00
14. ☐ 1970	KRONBORG		19.50–24.00
15. ☐ 1970	MARIBO		19.50–24.00
16. ☐ 1970	VIBORG		19.50–24.00
17. ☐ 1971	AARHUS		19.50–24.00
18. ☐ 1971	HADERSLEV		19.50–24.00
19. ☐ 1971	ODENSE		19.50–24.00
20. ☐ 1971	RIBE		19.50–24.00
21. ☐ 1971	ROSKILDE		19.50–24.00

ROYAL DOULTON
(England/U. S. A.)

An old and respected name in the field of porcelain and ceramics, Royal Doulton is best known for producing "Toby" jugs in the style of the Staffordshire eighteenth century English pieces.

Their unique collector's Christmas plates feature scenes of the Christmas holiday being celebrated in countries around the world. The first plate in the series depicts a traditional English family Christmas, complete with roast goose and plum pudding. The plates are executed in deep relief, with brightly colored, hand-painted scenes applied before final glazing and firing.

To provide collectors in the U.S. and Canada with a gallery of decorative art masterpieces on Royal Doulton fine bone china, Doulton and Co. has established "Collectors International." Under this program, Doulton has already commissioned a number of well-known artists to create art especially designed for reproduction on Royal Doulton plates. The first issue of this decorative art concept depicts Edna Hibel's *Colette and Child*; it has been extremely well received in the market. Miss Hibel will paint additional mother and child studies for the collection.

Planned for the fall is a biblical series by Fray Gabriel, a Mexican Benedictine monk widely known for his expressionistic art and architecture. This series, to be introduced in pairs, will depict scenes from the Old and New Testaments.

Subsequent additions to the Collectors International gallery are expected to include works by Dong Kingman, LeRoy Neiman, Robert Lougheed, Marguerite Hahn Vidal, Charles Banks Wilson, John Stobart, and Salvador Dali, each of whom is a specialist in a particular area of artistic expression.

Some works will be presented as individual pieces, while others will appear in a series. All editions will consist of signed works. Editions will be of varying quantities, with the edition limit carefully recorded on the fired backstamp.

Christmas Around the World Plate, 8"

1. ☐ 1972— FIRST ISSUE CHRISTMAS IN ENGLAND   40.00–50.00
2. ☐ 1973   CHRISTMAS IN MEXICO   45.00–55.00

Collectors International Plate, 8"

[For color illustrations, see page 66.]

3. ☐ 1973   MOTHER'S DAY—
                          Colette and Child   125.00–200.00

ROYAL IRISH SILVER, LTD.

(Ireland)

In keeping with the ancient Irish tradition of craftsmanship and artistic excellence, the silver products of Royal Irish Silver, Ltd., are proudly offered to the American collector. Two series presently available are the St. Patrick's Cathedral (Dublin) Restoration plates and the Georgian Dublin plates.

The St. Patrick's Cathedral plates feature views of the cathedral, the cathedral seal, and a portrait of Jonathan Swift, who was dean from 1713 to 1745. Each edition is limited to 750 plates.

The Irish Georgian Society commissioned Royal Irish Silver to produce a series of silver plates decorated with six engravings of famous Dublin buildings; these were reproduced from engravings published in 1780 by Robert Peel and John Cash. The Georgian Society edition is also limited to 750 plates and will come out twice a year for a period of three years.

To mark the completion of Eamon de Valera's term of office as president of Ireland, Royal Irish Silver, Ltd., issued a commemorative silver plate in an edition of 2,500. All Royal Irish sterling silver plates weigh approximately ten ounces.

St. Patrick's Cathedral Plate, 9¼"

1. ☐ 1973	EXTERIOR OF THE CATHEDRAL	100.00
2. ☐ 1973	INTERIOR OF THE CATHEDRAL	Each*
3. ☐ 1973	CHAPTER SEAL OF THE CATHEDRAL	
4. ☐ 1973	PORTRAIT OF JONATHAN SWIFT	

---

* Prices quoted are approximate retail for plates in mint condition. Silver and gold plate prices subject to radical change due to price fluctuation of these metals. For explanation of A.B.P. (Average Buying Price) and Mint Condition see pages 9–11.

Georgian Dublin Plate, 9¼"

5. ☐ 1972	TRINITY COLLEGE, DUBLIN	90.00
6. ☐ 1972	DUBLIN CASTLE	Each
7. ☐ 1973	LORD POWERSCOURT'S HOUSE	
8. ☐ 1973	PARLIAMENT HOUSE	

Commemorative Plate, 11"

9. ☐ 1973	EAMON DE VALERA	175.00

5   **7**   **6**

ROYAL TETTAU

(Germany)

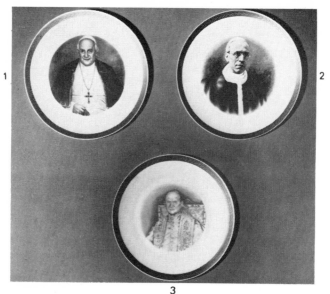

3

This Bavarian factory, the parent company of Royal Bayreuth (also listed in this book), was established in 1794. It has been responsible for the production of beautiful porcelain plates throughout its long and distinguished history. Outstanding popes are commemorated in its first limited edition collector's series, of which there are four pieces. 18k gold decorates the rim of each plate, which also features a color portrait of the man being thus honored. The pope's major goals are reflected in the form of an inscription on the back of each plate.

Each edition is limited to 5,000 pieces.

Great Popes Plate, 10½"

1. ☐ 1971— FIRST ISSUE	PAUL VI		40.00–90.00*
2. ☐ 1972.	JOHN XXIII		40.00–90.00
3. ☐ 1973	PIUS XII		115.00–125.00

* Prices quoted in book are approximate retail for plates in mint condition. For explanation of A.B.P. (Average Buying Price) and Mint Condition see pages 9–11.

ROYALE/GERMANIA CRYSTAL
(Germany)

4

Royale's limited edition items, in both porcelain and crystal, have been very popular among collectors. The porcelain plates are colored in several different shades of underglaze blue. The 1972 Mother's Day plate is fashioned in relief, as is the Father's Day plate and the 1971 Christmas plate. A pure white rabbit was introduced in the 1972 Easter plate. Each Easter (until 1982) a different sculpted rabbit will appear on Royale's Easter plate. The Christmas and Mother's Day plates appeared in editions of 6,000–10,000 (approximately) and the Father's Day of 4,000.

Royale's extremely fine crystal items, distributed under the name Royale/Germania, include an Annual plate and a Mother's Day series. These plates continue the centuries-old tradition of fine-cut crystal established in Royale's original Bohemian glass factory (which was moved to Bavaria after World War II). In 1970 the color used in the plate was blue; red was used for both series in 1971; green was the choice for 1972; and in 1973 the color was lilac.

All Royale/Germania crystal plates are lead crystal, copperwheel-engraved, numbered, and signed. The Annual plates are in editions of about 600 each, and the Mother's Day series has been 250, 750, and 600 plates respectively.

Christmas Plate, 7½"

1. ⊐ 1969— FIRST ISSUE	CHRISTMAS FAIR	50.00–80.00
2. ☐ 1970	MASS AT KALUNBORG CHURCH	12.50–25.00
3. ☐ 1971	SNOW ON THE ROOFTOPS	18.00–22.00
4. ☐ 1972	REINDEER IN SNOW	20.00–40.00
5. ☐ 1973	FEEDING THE DUCKS	20.00–24.00

181

Easter Plate, 7½"

6. ☐ 1972— FIRST ISSUE EASTER RABBIT   17.50–22.50
7. ☐ 1973   EASTER RABBIT   20.00–25.00

9

10

Mother's Day Plate, 7½"

8. ☐ 1970— FIRST ISSUE SWAN AND BROOD   40.00–50.00
9. ☐ 1971   DOE AND FAWN   16.00–25.00
10. ☐ 1972   RABBIT FAMILY   16.00–25.00
11. ☐ 1973   MOTHER OWL AND FAMILY   24.00–50.00

14

Mother's Day Germania Crystal Plate, 6¼"

12. ☐ 1971— FIRST ISSUE ROSES, RED   450.00–600.00
13. ☐ 1972   ELEPHANT MOTHER AND BABY,
                     DARK GREEN   200.00–250.00
14. ☐ 1973   KOALA BEAR AND CUB, LILAC 225.00–275.00

17   18

Father's Day Plate, 7½"

15. ☐ 1970—	FIRST ISSUE	SAILING SHIP	15.00–25.00
16. ☐ 1971		MAN FISHING	14.50–17.50
17. ☐ 1972		MOUNTAIN CLIMBER	16.00–30.00
18. ☐ 1973		AROUND THE CAMPFIRE	18.00–30.00

Astronaut Plate, 7½"

19. ☐ 1970	LANDING ON THE MOON	50.00–80.00

Game Plate, 12½"

20. ☐ 1972—	FIRST ISSUE	TWO SETTERS	
		POINTING QUAIL	250.00–325.00

Annual Germania Crystal Plate, 7½"

[For color illustrations, see page 63.]

21. ☐ 1970—	FIRST ISSUE	ORCHID, BLUE	450.00–650.00
22. ☐ 1971		CYCLAMEN, RED	200.00–250.00
23. ☐ 1972		SILVER THISTLE, GREEN	250.00–275.00
24. ☐ 1973		TULIPS, LILAC	275.00–325.00

SCHUMANN

(Germany)

1   2

After producing fine ware for ninety years, this Bavarian china company decided to enter the limited edition collector's field in 1970. Great composers are commemorated on their first series of plates. Their annual Christmas plate, decorated in cobalt blue underglaze, was first issued in 1971.

Christmas Plate, 7½"

1. ☐ 1971— FIRST ISSUE	SNOW SCENE	12.00–15.00*
2. ☐ 1972	DEER IN THE SNOW	12.00–15.00
3. ☐ 1973	RURAL WINTER SCENE	15.00–20.00

Great Composers, 7½"

4. ☐ 1970— FIRST ISSUE	BEETHOVEN	15.00–20.00
5. ☐ 1972	MOZART	15.00–20.00

* Prices quoted in book are approximate retail for plates in mint condition. For explanation of A.B.P. (Average Buying Price) and Mint Condition see pages 9–11.

SEVEN SEAS TRADERS

(Germany)

3

All of these Seven Seas Traders limited edition plates are decorated through a process of overglaze transfer in a variety of attractive colors. Their popular "Scandinavian Girl" Mother's Day plate was issued in 1972. Before man had actually landed on the moon, the company had already issued their 1969 History plate (in one of its two versions), without a flag or the date. Seven Seas issues two popular varieties of Christmas plates: a Christmas Carol plate and a New World Christmas plate. The variety of plate series produced by Seven Seas Traders shows the great creative innovations of this company. The Christmas Carol and History plates are 2,000–4,000 each edition, the Oberammergau plate is 2,500, and the Mother's Day and New World Christmas plates are 1,500 each edition.

Christmas Carol Plate, 7½"

[*For color illustrations, see page 168.*]

1. ☐ 1970— FIRST ISSUE	I HEARD THE BELLS ON CHRISTMAS DAY	18.00–30.00
2. ☐ 1971	OH TANNENBAUM	18.00–30.00
3. ☐ 1972	DECK THE HALLS	20.00–24.00
4. ☐ 1973	O HOLY NIGHT	20.00–24.00

New World Christmas Plate, 7½"

5. ☐ 1970— FIRST ISSUE	HOLY FAMILY OF CHRISTENDOM	14.50–20.00
6. ☐ 1971	THE KING IS HERE	14.50–20.00
7. ☐ 1972	AND SHEPHERDS WATCHED	20.00–24.00

Mother's Day Plate, 7½"

8. ☐ 1970— FIRST ISSUE	GIRL OF ALL NATIONS	18.00–30.00
9. ☐ 1971	SHARING CONFIDENCES	14.50–25.00
10. ☐ 1972	SCANDINAVIAN GIRL	14.50–25.00
11. ☐ 1973	ALL-AMERICAN GIRL	18.00–30.00

History Plate, 7½"

[For color illustrations, see page 168.]

12. ☐ 1969— FIRST ISSUE	LANDING ON THE MOON— APOLLO 11-"A"	100.00–150.00
13. ☐ 1969	SAME, NO FLAG OR DATE	30.00–50.00
14. ☐ 1970	A YEAR OF CRISIS	18.00–30.00
15. ☐ 1971	TRAVEL ON THE MOON	15.00–25.00
16. ☐ 1972	APOLLO 17	15.00–25.00
17. ☐ 1973	PEACE PLATE	15.00–25.00

Oberammergau Plate, 7½"

18. ☐ 1970	CARRYING THE CROSS	30.00–40.00

7

6

8

10

11

14

16

17

SILVER CITY

(U. S. A.)

5

By means of a special process, sterling silver is added to the plates of fine crystal that this company produces, making them both unusual and distinctive. Through the addition of a thin plating of rhodium over the silver, they are permanently preserved and tarnish-proof. Silver City produces two series of limited edition plates under the name Sterling America, which are listed in this book. This third series is produced under its own name.

Christmas Plate

1. ☐ 1969— FIRST ISSUE	WINTER SCENE, 12″	20.00–24.00*
2. ☐ 1970	WATER MILL, 12″	17.50–22.50
3. ☐ 1971	SKATING SCENE, 10″	17.50–22.50
4. ☐ 1972	LOGGING IN WINTER, 10″	18.50–24.00
5. ☐ 1973	SPIRIT OF '76, 10″	25.00–30.00

* *Prices quoted are approximate retail for plates in mint condition. Silver and gold plate prices subject to radical change due to price fluctuation of these metals. For explanation of A.B.P. (Average Buying Price) and Mint Condition see pages 9–11.*

SILVER CREATIONS LTD.
(U. S. A.)

The life of Sir Winston Churchill is the subject of a five-year series by Silver Creations. Churchill's nephew, John Spencer Churchill, executed the initial work on the series; he had been the constant painting companion of the great statesman. Sir Winston Churchill's most important message to the world occurred at twelve noon. To commemorate this event the first issue is named "The Hour of Decision."

More than 5,000 grains of solid sterling silver are used for each plate; they are struck in bas-relief and measure more than 9″ in diameter. A limited number are available in proof. Churchill's daughter Sarah designed the presentation case for each of the annual works.

The second creation of this company is the Americana series, a limited edition issued in 1973. It illustrates the world-famous Anheuser-Busch Clydesdale horses. The Busch family stables serve as background. The plates, sculpted in bas-relief, are produced in solid sterling silver.

Churchill Heritage Plate, 9″

1. 1972	PORTRAIT—THE HOUR OF DECISION		
☐		STERLING SILVER	175.00–250.00*
☐		STERLING SILVER PROOF	575.00
2. 1973	YALTA CONFERENCE		
☐		STERLING SILVER	150.00–175.00
☐		STERLING SILVER PROOF	575.00

* *Prices quoted are approximate retail for plates in mint condition. Silver and gold plate prices subject to radical change due to price fluctuation of these metals. For explanation of A.B.P. (Average Buying Price) and Mint Condition see pages 9–11.*

L. E. SMITH GLASS/WENDELL AUGUST FORGE

(U. S. A.)

2   1

The L. E. Smith Glass Company, well-known as a glass manufacturer, also produces items in silver and pewter. Amethyst carnival glass, with the designs in relief, are used for its Christmas, Coin and Famous American plates. The 1971 Christmas plate is bordered with holly wreaths; the 1972 Christmas plate and the coin and glass plates have a scalloped border.

Both the pewter and silver plates in these series are handmade at the Wendell August Forge in Grove City, Pennsylvania. Each silver plate is individually numbered and registered. The designs are in sharply detailed relief. The edges are irregular and serrated. Pewter plates were issued in quantities of 5,000 each. Sterling silver plates, which were issued in quantities of 500 each, weigh seventeen ounces.

The glass plates appeared in issues of 5,000 each except for the first two, in the "Famous American" series, which were 2,500 each.

Christmas Plate, 8¼"

---

1. ☐ 1971— FIRST ISSUE FAMILY AT CHRISTMAS,
                                          CARNIVAL GLASS   10.00
2. ☐ 1972   FLYING ANGEL, CARNIVAL GLASS   10.00

190

Coin Plate, 9"

3. ☐ 1971— FIRST ISSUE REPLICA OF THE SILVER DOLLAR,
   CARNIVAL GLASS   10.00

8   9

Famous American Plate, 9"

4. ☐ 1971— FIRST ISSUE JOHN F. KENNEDY, CARNIVAL GLASS   10.00
5. ☐ 1971   ABRAHAM LINCOLN, CARNIVAL GLASS   10.00
6. ☐ 1972   JEFFERSON DAVIS, CARNIVAL GLASS   10.00
7. ☐ 1973   ROBERT E. LEE, CARNIVAL GLASS   12.00

Wendell August Presidential Plate, 9"

8. 1971— FIRST ISSUE   JOHN F. KENNEDY,
   ☐   PEWTER   40.00
   ☐   STERLING SILVER   200.00–250.00*
9. 1972   ABRAHAM LINCOLN,
   ☐   PEWTER   40.00
   ☐   STERLING SILVER   200.00–250.00

* Prices quoted are approximate retail for plates in mint condition. Silver and gold plate prices subject to radical change due to price fluctuation of these metals. For explanation of A.B.P. (Average Buying Price) and Mint Condition see pages 9–11.

10

11

12

Great Moments in History Plate, 9"

10.	1972— FIRST ISSUE	LANDING OF THE PILGRIMS,	
☐		PEWTER	40.00
☐		STERLING SILVER	200.00–250.00
11.	1973	THE FIRST THANKSGIVING,	
☐		PEWTER	40.00
☐		STERLING SILVER	200.00–250.00

Wings of Man Plate, 9"

12.	1972— FIRST ISSUE	SHIPS OF COLUMBUS—	
		NINA, PINTA, SANTA MARIA,	
☐		PEWTER	40.00
☐		STERLING SILVER	200.00–250.00
13.	1973	CONESTOGA WAGON,	
☐		PEWTER	40.00
☐		STERLING SILVER	200.00–250.00

SPODE

(England)

Josiah Spode, who founded this company, began as an apprentice at the age of sixteen. Thirty years later, after he had learned every aspect of his trade, he became the owner of the "Twelve Acres" pottery factory, located in Stoke. It was renamed Spode Works in 1776. Among the many contributions made by Spode Works since it began operations are the introduction (to Staffordshire) of underglaze blue, the perfected process of underglaze printing, and the perfecting of bone china. The last is the most significant, for the formula created by Josiah Spode is still being used today.

Josiah Spode was personally responsible for his company's innovations; after his death his descendants helped to shape the business for several generations. Spode had taken on a partner, William Copeland, whose descendants also helped shape the company. Many craftsmen working for Spode Works today are descendants of Josiah Spode.

Old English carols are commemorated on the Christmas plate. Square-shaped Lowestoft china is used for the Peace plate, designed by Cecil Beaton in a butterfly pattern. The Imperial Plate of Persia was issued in 1971 to commemorate 2,500 years of Persian monarchy. This beautiful plate is decorated in 22k gold and rich enamels on white bone china. All of the items made by Spode are produced in limited editions. The Commemoratives listed are all under 10,000 each.

Christmas Plate, 8"

1. ☐ 1970—FIRST ISSUE	PARTRIDGE IN A PEAR TREE	40.00
2. ☐ 1971	IN HEAVEN THE ANGELS WERE SINGING	35.00
3. ☐ 1972	WE SAW THREE SHIPS A-SAILING	35.00
4. ☐ 1973	WE THREE KINGS OF ORIENT ARE	40.00

Ray Harm American Songbird Plates

Ray Harm, the famous wildlife artist and naturalist who makes his home in the mountains of Kentucky, has designed a limited edition of American Songbird collector plates. Spode has produced these charming true-to-life bird paintings in beautiful bone china English porcelain plates.

5. ☐	TOWHEE AND RED-BELLIED WOODPECKER	225.00
6. ☐	AMERICAN GOLDFINCH AND WINTER HEN	140.00
7. ☐ 1970	WESTERN TANAGER AND CAROLINA CHICKADEE	110.00
to		
8. ☐ 1972	EASTERN BLUEBIRD AND ROSE-BREASTED GROSBEAK	65.00
9. ☐	CARDINAL AND BARN SWALLOWS	65.00
10. ☐	EASTERN MOCKINGBIRD AND STELLAR'S JAY	65.00
	COMPLETE SET	650.00–800.00

Commemorative Plate

[For color illustrations, see page 173.]

11. ☐ 1970   BEATON'S *Peace Plate*, 8½"   20.00
12. ☐ 1970   MAYFLOWER PLATE, 10½"   130.00
13. ☐ 1970   DICKENS PLATE, 10½"   70.00
14. ☐ 1971   CHURCHILL PLATE, 10½"   100.00
15. ☐ 1971   IMPERIAL PLATE OF PERSIA, 10½"   125.00
16. ☐ 1972   PASSOVER PLATE, 10½"   42.50
17. ☐ 1972   CUTTY-SARK PLATE, 10½"   35.00

12

15

16

ST. AMAND

(France)

1

2

An old (over 200 years) and respected name in French faience, St. Amand introduced the first issue of their typical amandine blue-grey bas-relief annual plate to the American market in 1970 in a limited edition of 10,000 pieces.

A second issue was released in 1971. It depicts two deer in a woodsy glen, executed in a delicate amandine blue-grey color.

St. Amand Annual Plate, 9½"

1. ☐ 1970— FIRST ISSUE	TWO BIRDS IN A TREE	8.00–10.00*
2. ☐ 1971	TWO DEER IN THE WOODS	7.50–9.50

* *Prices quoted in book are approximate retail for plates in mint condition. For explanation of A.B.P. (Average Buying Price) and Mint Condition see pages 9–11.*

FRANZ STANEK/WARA INTERCONTINENTAL

(Germany)

Franz Stanek, a Czechoslovakian refugee of the 1968 invasion, is one of the few remaining masters of the art of copper-wheel engraving, using copper wheels of many shapes and sizes to deep-engrave intricate designs on crystal. This takes time and great skill—it took Stanek about forty-five hours to create his Moon Landing plate, commissioned by Wara Intercontinental. His works include commissions from Queen Elizabeth of England and Emperor Haile Selassie of Ethiopia.

The Santa Maria plate is deep-engraved by hand into dark ruby overlay crystal containing over 24% lead monoxide, used only for the finest crystalware. The Mayflower plate is done the same way in cobalt blue overlay crystal of the same superb quality.

The plates, numbered and signed by Stanek, are accompanied by a signed certificate of authenticity. Wara Intercontinental is the sole distributor of Stanek plates, which were issued in extremely limited editions: 150 for the 1970 plate, and 60 each for the other two plates.

Franz Stanek Plate

1. ☐ 1970— FIRST ISSUE	MAN'S FIRST MOON LANDING, 12″	1,200.00
2. ☐ 1971	SANTA MARIA, COLUMBUS'S FLAGSHIP, 11″	650.00
3. ☐ 1972	MAYFLOWER, PILGRIMS' SHIP, 11″	600.00

1

3

STERLING AMERICA/
SILVER CITY
(U. S. A.)

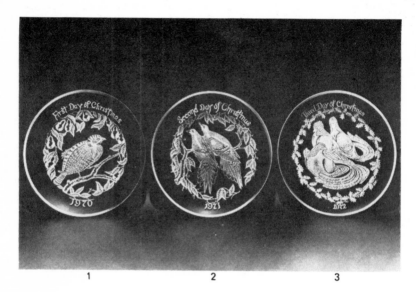

Manufactured by Silver City, these unusual limited edition plates are made of fine crystal with designs in sterling silver. The beautiful balance struck between the relatively simple pictures and their extremely fine and exact detail give these plates an added distinctiveness. To make them permanently lustrous and nontarnishable, the silver is coated with rhodium.

Christmas Song Plate, 8"

1. ☐ 1970— FIRST ISSUE	PARTRIDGE IN A PEAR TREE	23.50–27.50*
2. ☐ 1971	TWO TURTLE DOVES	23.50–27.50
3. ☐ 1972	THREE FRENCH HENS	21.00–24.00
4. ☐ 1973	FOUR COLLY BIRDS	20.00–24.00

* *Prices quoted are approximate retail for plates in mint condition. Silver and gold plate prices subject to radical change due to price fluctuation of these metals. For explanation of A.B.P. (Average Buying Price) and Mint Condition see pages 9–11.*

Christmas Customs Plate, 8"

5. ☐ 1970—	FIRST ISSUE	BRINGING HOME THE YULE LOG	25.50–27.50
6. ☐ 1971		CHRISTMAS IN HOLLAND	23.50–27.50
7. ☐ 1972		CHRISTMAS IN NORWAY	21.00–24.00
8. ☐ 1973		CHRISTMAS IN GERMANY	20.00–22.50

Mother's Day Plate, 8"

9. ☐ 1971—	FIRST ISSUE	MARE AND FOAL	23.50–27.50
10. ☐ 1972		GREAT HORNED OWL	21.00–24.00
11. ☐ 1973		RACCOONS	20.00–22.50

STUMAR

(U. S. A.)

1

2

3

These limited edition items from Pennsylvania's Glenview Pottery use Pennsylvania Dutch themes as their subject. The Christmas and Mother's Day plates are hand-painted in deep shades of red, green, brown, and yellow, with touches of other colors; delicate browns are used as background. The designs are in low relief.

Artists at Glenview Pottery individually design two distinctive, personalized gifts to commemorate either a wedding or an anniversary. Each is completely hand-carved and hand-decorated in beautiful colors. The design features a pair of Distelfinks, the Pennsylvania Dutch good-luck bird, surrounded by tulips.

Christmas Plate, 8 ¼"

1. ☐ 1970— FIRST ISSUE	ANGEL	15.00–20.00
2. ☐ 1971	THE OLD CANAL	10.00–12.00
3. ☐ 1972	COUNTRYSIDE	10.00–12.00
4. ☐ 1973	FRIENDSHIP	10.00–12.00

5   6

7

Mother's Day Plate, 8¼"

[For color illustrations, see page 173.]

5. ☐	1971— FIRST ISSUE	MOTHER AND DAUGHTER	8.00–10.00
6. ☐	1972	CHILDREN	8.00–10.00
7. ☐	1973	MOTHER SEWING QUILT	10.00–12.00

Anniversary Plate, 8½"

8. ☐	AS PER ORDER	(THE CUSTOMER PROVIDES FULL NAME OF HUSBAND AND WIFE, DATE OF MARRIAGE, AND ANNIVERSARY NUMBER.) 15.00

Wedding Plate, 8½"

9. ☐	AS PER ORDER	(SAME AS ABOVE, WITH THE EXCEPTION OF THE ANNIVERSARY NUMBER.) 15.00

SVEND-JENSEN/DÉSIRÉE

(Denmark)

1   2   4

These attractive collectible plates are designed and distributed exclusively in the United States by Svend-Jensen of Denmark, Inc. They are produced by the Désirée porcelain factory in Denmark. This modern factory, founded in 1966, is located only a few miles from the Danish capital of Copenhagen. The Christmas plates produced by Désirée are based upon Hans Christian Andersen's world-famous fairy tales. Well-known Danish artists have captured the spirit and thought behind these fairy tales, disclosing a message of life in which man's imagination triumphs over reality. This message of inspiration and hope will continue to appear once each year.

The Svend-Jensen plates are made in the time-honored tradition of the Copenhagen Christmas plates. Each is hand-painted in the classic Copenhagen blue hues on a carefully engraved bas-relief porcelain surface. It is then fired at an exceptionally high temperature (over 2,600 degrees) to permanently preserve the texture and painting under a crystal-clear glaze. The plates are produced in very limited quantities; the molds are destroyed each year to ensure that the plates will never be reproduced at a future date. There is a very high standard set for quality. Only first-quality plates are shipped to North America. Out of total production, two thirds of their plates are first quality, one third seconds; the seconds are never used for export.

5

3

6

7

8

Christmas Plate, 7″

[For color illustrations, see page 64.]

1. ☐ 1970— FIRST ISSUE	HANS CHRISTIAN ANDERSEN'S HOUSE	50.00–75.00
2. ☐ 1971	THE LITTLE MATCH GIRL	20.00–40.00
3. ☐ 1972	MERMAID OF COPENHAGEN	20.00–40.00
4. ☐ 1973	THE FIR TREE	20.00–25.00

Mother's Day Plate, 7″

5. ☐ 1970— FIRST ISSUE	A BOUQUET FOR MOTHER	20.00–30.00
6. ☐ 1971	MOTHER'S LOVE	22.00–30.00
7. ☐ 1972	A CHILD IN ARMS	18.00–25.00
8. ☐ 1973	FLOWERS FOR MOTHER	22.00–30.00

Father's Day Plate, 7″

9. ☐ 1972	FATHER'S JOY	18.00–22.00

TAYLOR-SMITH & TAYLOR
(U. S. A.)

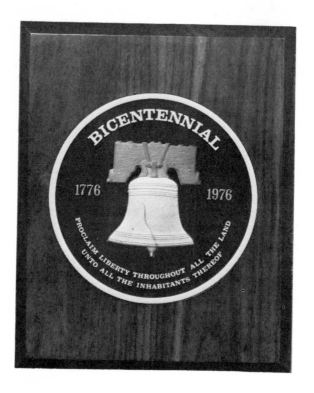

The Liberty Bell, sculpted in three dimensions, graces the center of this handsome 10½" plate. This plate of fine ivory clay is decorated in deep blue and white with real gold trim.

Bicentennial Plate, 10½"

[For color illustrations, see page 173.]

☐ 1973   LIBERTY BELL   10.00*

* Prices quoted in book are approximate retail for plates in mint condition. For explanation of A.B.P. (Average Buying Price) and Mint Condition see pages 9–11.

VAL SAINT LAMBERT

(Belgium)

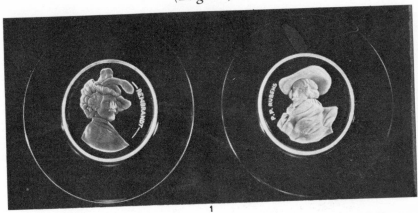

1

Art glass collectors know this company as the producer of fine cameo glass during the Art Nouveau period. The style of Val Saint Lambert is similar to Lalique.

The home of this factory is a 750-year-old abbey originally dedicated to Saint Lambert. The Cristalleries Du Val-Saint-Lambert, now almost 150 years old, has been recognized as a producer of flawless, clear crystal and beautiful designs. Famous painters are honored on their Old Masters plates. These plates feature deeply engraved designs with acid finishes. Another series they produce, the American Heritage plates, are copper-wheel engraved hand-cut. The plates in both of these series are individually inscribed and strictly limited.

Old Masters Plate, 8"

			Set of 2
1. ☐ 1968— FIRST ISSUE	RUBENS, REMBRANDT		90.00*
2. ☐ 1969	VAN GOGH, VAN DYCK		60.00–75.00
3. ☐ 1970	DA VINCI, MICHELANGELO		60.00–75.00
4. ☐ 1971	EL GRECO, GOYA		50.00–65.00
5. ☐ 1972	REYNOLDS, GAINSBOROUGH		50.00–65.00

* Prices quoted in book are approximate retail for plates in mint condition. For explanation of A.B.P. (Average Buying Price) and Mint Condition see pages 9–11.

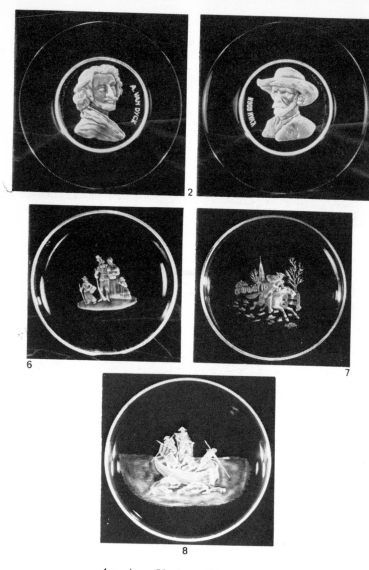

American Heritage Plate, 12"

6. ☐ 1969— FIRST ISSUE PILGRIM FATHERS   400.00–600.00
7. ☐ 1970   PAUL REVERE'S RIDE   150.00–250.00
8. ☐ 1971   WASHINGTON CROSSING
                           THE DELAWARE   150.00–250.00

VAN GOGH/CREATIVE WORLD
(Italy)

This unique series was created and distributed by Veneto Flair, which has an extensive list in this book.

Scenes from Vincent Van Gogh's paintings are re-created on these square-shaped porcelain plates, made by Creative World, the same production source for all the issues of Veneto Flair.

Van Gogh Plate, 8"

1. ☐ 1971— FIRST ISSUE	DRAWBRIDGE	12.50
2. ☐ 1972	NIGHT CAFE	12.50
3. ☐ 1973	FISHING BOATS	12.00

VENETO FLAIR/CREATIVE WORLD

(Italy)

All the items produced by Veneto Flair, a company which issues a number of collector plate series, are manufactured by Italy's Creative World. The first plate issued by Veneto Flair appeared in 1970 and is known as the "Bellini Madonna." Only 500 plates were issued. This plate originally sold for $37.50 retail; it now costs between $400 and $650. All Veneto Flair plates are issued in editions of 2,000 or less. They are true limited editions.

Most Veneto Flair plates are made of majolica (a thick, heavy faience) with a gold or silver border. They resemble fine paintings in their magnificent coloring and texture. Each plate is handmade —turned on a potter's wheel and then hand-etched—individually signed and numbered.

"The Last Supper" is one of Veneto Flair's newest majolica series. Each of the first four plates features three Apostles; the fifth plate bears a portrait of Christ. The Easter series is also executed in majolica. A "Four Seasons" sequence has been designed with a sterling silver border. The company has also produced first issues of sterling silver Christmas and Valentine plate series. A venetian border rims the Valentine's Day plate; the Christmas plate has a hand-engraved edge.

Madonna Plate, 8½"

1. ☐ 1970— ONLY ISSUE   BELLINI MADONNA   400.00–650.00

3   **10**

Ceramic Christmas Plate, 8½"

2. ☐ 1971— FIRST ISSUE THREE KINGS		125.00–200.00
3. ☐ 1972 THREE SHEPHERDS		75.00–100.00
4. ☐ 1973 MADONNA AND CHILD		50.00–75.00

Silver Christmas Plate, 8½"

5. ☐ 1972— FIRST ISSUE MADONNA AND CHILD
OF THE BOOK   135.00–160.00

Silver Valentine Plate, 8½"

6. ☐ 1973— FIRST ISSUE ROMEO AND JULIET   135.00–160.00

Easter Plate, 8½"

7. ☐ 1973— FIRST ISSUE RABBITS   60.00–90.00

Mother's Day Plate, 8½"

8. ☐ 1972— FIRST ISSUE MOTHER AND CHILD   100.00–175.00
9. ☐ 1973   MADONNA AND CHILD   55.00–100.00

Stained Glass Plate, 8½"

For color illustration, see page 174.

10. ☐ 1973— FIRST ISSUE MADONNA AND CHILD   115.00–150.00

11

Last Supper Plate, 8½"

11. ☐	1973— FIRST ISSUE	#1 THREE APOSTLES	70.00–100.00
☐		#2 THREE APOSTLES	Each
☐		#3 THREE APOSTLES	
☐		#4 THREE APOSTLES	
☐		#5 PORTRAIT OF CHRIST	
☐		COMPLETE SET	750.00–1000.00

Four Seasons Plate, 8½"

12. ☐	1972— FIRST ISSUE	FALL	125.00
13. ☐		WINTER	125.00
14. ☐		SPRING	125.00
15. ☐		SUMMER	125.00
		COMPLETE SET	500.00

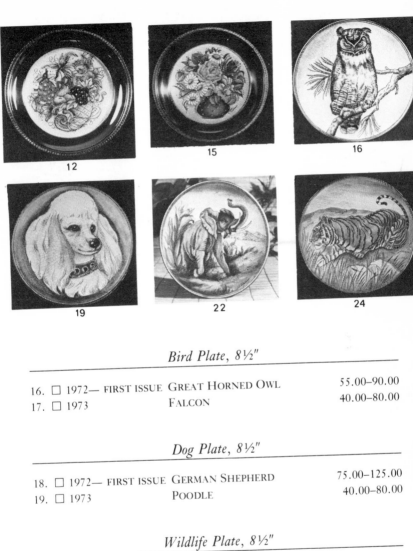

12 15 16

19 22 24

Bird Plate, 8½"

16. ☐ 1972—	FIRST ISSUE	GREAT HORNED OWL	55.00–90.00
17. ☐ 1973		FALCON	40.00–80.00

Dog Plate, 8½"

18. ☐ 1972—	FIRST ISSUE	GERMAN SHEPHERD	75.00–125.00
19. ☐ 1973		POODLE	40.00–80.00

Wildlife Plate, 8½"

[For color illustrations, see page 171.]

21. ☐ 1971—	FIRST ISSUE	STAG	375.00–500.00
22. ☐ 1971—	FIRST ISSUE	ELEPHANT	150.00–250.00
23. ☐ 1972		PUMA	50.00–85.00
24. ☐ 1973		TIGER	45.00–65.00

WEDGWOOD

(England)

1

2

Josiah Wedgwood founded this firm in 1759. He personally developed many of his company's early processes and materials. In 1774 he perfected a hard, unglazed stoneware, which he subsequently named "jasperware"—probably the most famous discovery that this imaginative and innovative potter ever made. In 1768 he perfected black basalt, an unglazed, fine-grained stoneware possessing a deep black color.

Wedgwood has become so popular that it is considered by many people to be synonymous with jasperware. It is best known in sky blue, although it has also been made in green, black, cobalt blue, and lavender, as well as other colors. The classic appearance of cameos is captured in the applied white jasper relief decorations.

America receives about 60% of Wedgwood's total production. This is exported from Barlaston, England, where Wedgwood moved in 1940. They produced their first Christmas plate in 1969 to celebrate the bicentennial of the founding of their original factory.

For their early designs, Wedgwood used the works of such famous eighteenth century artists as William Blake, John Flaxman, and Lady Elizabeth Templetown. Some of these are still used in the many pieces produced by Wedgwood. In addition to collector plates, they also make ashtrays, candy dishes, jugs, medallions, coasters, vases and other items.

The various Wedgwood collector plate series are so varied in theme and color that descriptive notes for them are included with the price listings below.

3   **4**

Christmas Plate, 8"

Wedgwood's Christmas plates illustrate famous English monuments. The mold for the fifth in the series, the 1973 "Tower of London" plate, was destroyed December 31, 1973; production subsequently ceased.

1. ☐ 1969— FIRST ISSUE	WINDSOR CASTLE	175.00–275.00*
2. ☐ 1970	TRAFALGAR SQUARE	25.00–40.00
3. ☐ 1971	PICADILLY CIRCUS	35.00–50.00
4. ☐ 1972	ST. PAUL'S CATHEDRAL	35.00–50.00
5. ☐ 1973	THE TOWER OF LONDON	50.00–75.00

Mother's Day Plate, 6½"

Wedgwood issued its first Mother's Day plate in 1971; it reproduced a design of 1780 by Lady Elizabeth Templetown in black basalt. The second, which originally retailed at $20, was "The Sewing Lesson"; fashioned of green and white jasperware, it used a 1795 design by Miss Emma Crewe. The 1973 plate, "The Baptism of Achilles," is a Wedgwood design dating from the 1780s; it contains the world-famous pale blue jasperware with white bas-relief ornaments. Classical laurel-leaf borders encircle all three Mother's Day plates.

6. ☐ 1971— FIRST ISSUE	SPORTIVE LOVE	25.00
7. ☐ 1972	THE SEWING LESSON	25.00
8. ☐ 1973	THE BAPTISM OF ACHILLES	20.00

8   11

Child's Day (Children's Story) Plate, 6"

Stories by Hans Christian Andersen are illustrated on both the
Child's Day plate, which is made for U.S. distribution, and the
Children's Story plate intended for European distribution. These
plates are made of Queensware, a white glazed china, plus overglaze
decoration.

9. ☐ 1971— FIRST ISSUE THE SANDMAN
10. ☐ 1972   THE TINDER BOX   9.50–12.50
11. ☐ 1973   THE EMPEROR'S NEW CLOTHES 8.00–10.00
                                                                8.00–10.00

Calendar Plate, 10"

12   13

Wedgwood held a competition at the Royal College of Art in 1971
for the right to design this series. It was won by twenty-three-year-
old Keith Manuel, who has designed all three plates since the first
1971 issue. The plates are of white glazed Queensware and are
decorated in colors. All three plates carry zodiac motifs as well as the
names of the months.

12. ☐ 1971— FIRST ISSUE PASTORAL CHERUBS
13. ☐ 1972   ZODIAC   18.50–25.00
14. ☐ 1973   BUTTERFLIES   17.50–25.00
                                                        15.00–22.50

15

16

17

American Independence Plate, 8"

Josiah Wedgwood strongly supported the American Revolution. Since the first export of Wedgwood to America, American commemorative ware has been produced by the company. Two series begun especially for the bicentennial are the American Independence plates and the State Seal "compotiers" or fruit saucers. The American Independence series consists of six plates in blue and white jasperware illustrating events from American history that led to independence. The thirteen stars on the border of each plate represent the thirteen original colonies. The plates will be issued until 1976, when the series will be complete. Each plate in the series is limited to 5,000.

15. ☐ 1972	BOSTON TEA PARTY	40.00–60.00
16. ☐ 1973	PAUL REVERE'S RIDE	35.00–55.00
17. ☐ 1973	BATTLE OF CONCORD	30.00–50.00

State Seal Plate, 4½"

This series, like the American Independence series, consists of blue and white jasperware; it is limited to 5,000 items and will be complete in 1976. The series is issued in thirteen sets, one for each of the thirteen states which supported the Declaration of Independence. One piece in each set features the seal of the state; the other bears the portrait of one of the signers from that state.

18. ☐	1972— FIRST ISSUE	VIRGINIA	25.00
19. ☐	1972	PENNSYLVANIA	Each set
20. ☐	1972	MASSACHUSETTS	
21. ☐	1972	NEW YORK	

Paolozzi Geometric Plate, 8"

Eduardo Paolozzi, the sculptor and graphic artist, designed a set of six brilliantly colored plates, produced in a limited edition of 200 sets in Wedgwood bone china. Paolozzi's interest in the relation of print graphics to technology is expressed in the series, as is indicated by the title.

22. ☐	1971	VARIATIONS ON A	Set of 6
		GEOMETRIC THEME	200.00

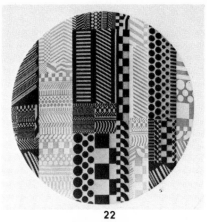

22

23

Commemorative Plate

During its long history, Wedgwood has designed and produced many commemorative issues. A few of the more recent ones are listed below. Green and white jasperware is used on the Shakespeare plate; the Apollo 11 plate consists of blue and white jasperware; and the Olympiad plate is made of black basalt trimmed in gold.

23. ☐ 1969	APOLLO 11, MAN ON THE MOON, 8″	30.00–50.00
24. ☐ 1970	350TH ANNIVERSARY OF THE MAYFLOWER, 10″	13.50
25. ☐ 1970	SHAKESPEARE/STRATFORD-ON-AVON, 8″	25.00–50.00
26. ☐ 1972	OLYMPIAD/MUNICH, 6½″	15.00–25.00

THE WELLINGS MINT/
THE FRANKLIN MINT

(Canada)

2

The Wellings Mint is a Canadian subsidiary of The Franklin Mint. A sketch by A. Y. Jackson, Canada's foremost living artist, will be reproduced on limited edition plates each fall (until 1976) by the Wellings Mint. This ninety-year-old artist is the only surviving member of the Group of Seven, a revolutionary art movement which had an enormous influence on Canada's artistic tradition in our own century. A drawing by Jackson, created in 1934 while he was in a small Quebec village (the scene of numerous hiking and painting trips), was featured in the 1971 issue. The sterling silver issue was limited to 5,200 pieces; 160 were made in 18k gold.

The theme of the Wellings Mint's series of six sterling silver Mother's Day plates is "Children of Mankind." The first issue of these plates consists of a hand-engraved sketch by Joe Rosenthal; it depicts a Cree Indian girl rocking her baby brother in a hammock.

Numbered certificates in hand-crafted presentation cases accompany both plates.

Gold and platinum plates may not be available.

Mother's Day Plate, 8″

1. 1972— FIRST ISSUE   LULLABY,
   ☐   STERLING SILVER   100.00–125.00*
   ☐   18k GOLD   1250.00–1500.00

Annual Christmas—A. Y. Jackson Plate, 8″

2. 1971— FIRST ISSUE   HOUSES, ST. URBAIN,
   ☐   STERLING SILVER   125.00–150.00
   ☐   18k GOLD   1000.00–1350.00
   ☐   PLATINUM   10,000.00
3. ☐ 1972   A. Y. JACKSON PLATE,
                          STERLING SILVER   100.00–130.00

* *Prices quoted are approximate retail for plates in mint condition. Silver and gold plate prices subject to radical change due to price fluctuation of these metals. For explanation of A.B.P. (Average Buying Price) and Mint Condition see pages 9–11.*

WHEATON/NULINE GLASS

(U. S. A.)

Wheaton/Nuline is the company responsible for the production of the highly collectible Avon bottles. A decanter in honor of John F. Kennedy was the subject of their first series of limited edition bottles. This was followed by the creation of other presidential decanters and various commemorative bottle series. This, in turn, led to the production of their limited edition Presidential plates.

At the present time, Wheaton/Nuline is in the process of building a museum and antique village in their home town of Millville, New Jersey. Intended to be a visitor's paradise, this museum/village will have its employees dressed in authentic period costumes; they will give handcraft demonstrations.

Each issue in the "Presidential Plate" series is produced in turquoise blue glass.

Presidential Plate, 8"

[*For color illustrations, see page 167.*]

1. ☐ 1971–2	ADAMS (JOHN) TURQUOISE BLUE GLASS	
2. ☐ 1971–2	EISENHOWER	
3. ☐ 1971–2	HOOVER	
4. ☐ 1971–2	KENNEDY	
5. ☐ 1971–2	LINCOLN	6.00–10.00
6. ☐ 1971–2	MADISON	Each
7. ☐ 1971–2	MONROE	
8. ☐ 1971–2	ROOSEVELT (F. D.)	
9. ☐ 1971–2	TAFT	
10. ☐ 1971–2	VAN BUREN	
11. ☐ 1971–2	WASHINGTON	
12. ☐ 1971–2	WILSON	

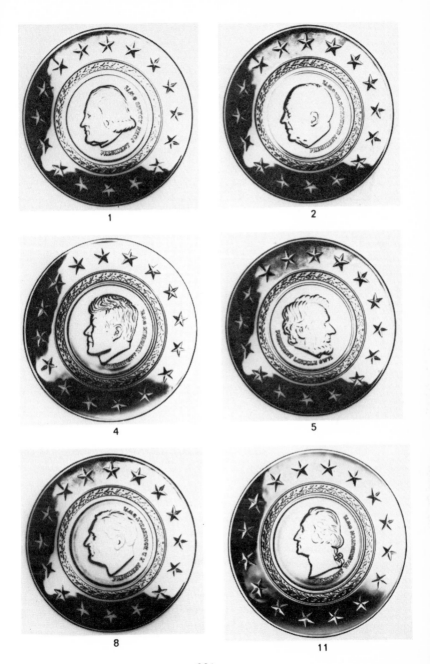

1

2

4

5

8

11

221

WILTON ARMETALE®

(U. S. A.)

2   3

    The Wilton Armetale metal foundry is located in Columbia, Pennsylvania, on the banks of the Susquehanna River. It is not far from historic Lancaster, the heart of Amish country. Using a special alloy (armetale®) first created at Wilton, this foundry hand-casts and polishes each issue. Colonial American metalware is re-created in the Wilton Alphabet plate. The Declaration of Independence and the Great Seal are the subjects—reproduced in full color—in the center of these lustrous armetale plates.

    Wilton has also produced a unique series of twelve armetale plates with ceramic inserts which reproduce the famous artwork of Kate Greenaway (1846–1901). Kate Greenaway, the daughter of a well-known engraver, was born in London. She possessed the innate ability to create art imbued with the spirit of gentleness and goodness; all her works reflect these qualities. She painted in watercolors, a medium which seemed perfectly suited to the delicate manner in which she portrayed children.

    Each plate bearing Kate Greenaway's art represents a different month of the year. The plates measure 10⅞″ in diameter. The back of each plate is stamped to indicate the month.

American History Plate, 11"

1. ☐ 1972	ALPHABET PLATE	10.00–12.50*
2. & 3. ☐ 1973	GREAT SEAL PLATE	15.00–20.00
4. ☐ 1973	DECLARATION OF	
	INDEPENDENCE PLATE	15.00–20.00

Kate Greenaway Plate, 10⅞"

5. ☐ 1973	JANUARY	
6. ☐ 1973	FEBRUARY	
7. ☐ 1973	MARCH	
8. ☐ 1973	APRIL	
9. ☐ 1973	MAY	
10. ☐ 1973	JUNE	16.00–20.00
11. ☐ 1973	JULY	Each
12. ☐ 1973	AUGUST	
13. ☐ 1973	SEPTEMBER	
14. ☐ 1973	OCTOBER	
15. ☐ 1973	NOVEMBER	
16. ☐ 1973	DECEMBER	

6

Prices quoted in book are approximate retail for plates in mint condition. For explanation of A.B.P. (Average Buying Price) and Mint Condition see pages 9–11.

VI

The History of Silver, Porcelain, and Glass

Silver

A person collecting silver today has a wide selection of silver art objects from which to choose. There is also a great range in price; even a person of average means will find many sterling silver items easily within his reach.

Silver is extremely popular among collectors. It is a good example of the ancient tradition of investment in precious metals for reasons of craftsmanship, natural beauty, and appreciation in value.

Gold and silver were frequently used by Egyptians, Assyrians, Phoenicians, Greeks, and Romans. Mention of gold and silver can be found scattered throughout the Old Testament.

Silver was, for a long time, used almost exclusively for utensils intended for religious purposes. More expensive articles of household decoration have also been fashioned of silver. Silver has often been inscribed for special occasions or used to commemorate important events; it has thus served as an historical record.

Until the end of the fifteenth century, silver was predominantly mined in Hungary, Transylvania, and Spain. With the discovery of the New World, however, enormous quantities of silver were uncovered in Peru and Mexico. Significant amounts can also be found in sea water.

Although silver is not as malleable as gold, it can be beaten into leaves that are a mere 1/100,000 of an inch thick. It can also be drawn into a wire that is finer than human hair. Silver is particularly appreciated for its ability to take on a brilliant polish.

In order to give silver the required degree of hardness, an alloy must be added. This alloy, usually copper, can be added to silver without materially affecting its color. There are 925 parts of silver and 75 parts of copper to every 1,000 parts of sterling silver.

Sterling was first stamped onto silver in 1850. Most pieces of silver which were made before 1850 are of "coin" quality. Electroplated ware made after 1840 is called plated silver. Plated silver is made by chemically depositing silver on a metal base. Its value depends on the depth of the plate and the taste and execution of the design.

Silver pieces made in England contain a very complex hallmark of symbols; these indicate the maker, his town, the date, and the silver content. Usually, silver pieces made in the U.S. are marked differ-

The origin of modern silver artifacts can be traced to the early days of banking houses in England, where the silversmith served as artistic metalcrafter as well as local banker.

ently (with a simple maker's mark), although some American makers mark their work in the same manner as their English counterparts.

Pieces of silver were once considered an index of symbolic and material wealth. Before the creation of savings banks, people would take their silver coins to a silversmith and have them converted into usable and decorative objects. Silver was therefore an investment; the early silversmiths played a role not unlike that of a banker. In colonial America, silversmiths were often prominent members of their community; Paul Revere is a notable example. Many of them were highly skilled, having undergone years of long apprenticeship.

There are liquid preparations which are used to remove tarnish from silver; the metal may either be dipped into the liquid in its entirety or a portion rubbed with the special solution. The original sheen on new silver can be preserved by lacquering, although when used to prevent tarnish on old silver the lacquering destroys the silver's patina. If silver is kept in a closed cabinet in which there is a piece of gum camphor (which can be purchased at any drug store), it will stay brighter for a longer period of time.

The natural beauty of silver has, since the earliest times, lent itself to the service of splendor. The fact that silver can be fashioned to suit the designs of the artist and craftsman has helped make it one of the best-known of the noble metals.

Porcelain

Porcelain originated sometime before the year 800. Some believe that it was first produced during the middle of the first century A.D., while others believe that it wasn't perfected until the year 618, when the T'ang period began.

Since prehistoric times, people have known the art of molding things out of clay and hardening them in fire. But it was the Chinese who first produced actual porcelain. This is the reason why the word "china" has often been used in place of porcelain.

The first European to see Chinese porcelain was Marco Polo. This event occurred between 1271 and 1295, when he visited the Court of China, although it wasn't until later that a limited amount was brought to Europe for wealthy buyers. Porcelain first became an article of commerce in 1497, when a sea route around the Cape of

Good Hope was discovered. During this lengthy interval, the Japanese and the Koreans had learned the secret of making porcelain.

Porcelain grew more and more popular. It was both decorative and useful. This induced European potters, glassmakers, and chemists to experiment in the hope of discovering the formula. They were unsuccessful. Although a number of soft-paste porcelain factories were established in France, the French factories didn't learn how to make hard-paste porcelain until the second half of the eighteenth century.

An alchemist named Johann Friedrich Boettger was the first man in the Western world to make actual porcelain (in 1709). The European nobility were the greatest collectors of Chinese porcelains. It was therefore under the patronage of August the Strong, Elector of Saxony, that Boettger worked. A porcelain factory at Meissen, a few miles from Dresden (in Saxony), grew out of his discovery. Countries all over the European continent eventually produced porcelain.

Strangely enough, the porcelain imported from China showed a marked European influence, while the early pieces made in Europe reflected a strong Chinese influence, both in form and decoration. Beginning in the mid-1700s, a huge trade in Oriental export porcelain developed; it was made to special order.

In the late 1820s, the Philadelphian William Tucker was responsible for the first major production of porcelain in America. Most porcelain used in America was imported from England, France, and Germany, however. This is still the case.

Hard-paste or true porcelain is white, acid-resistant, fine-textured, hard, and a low heat conductor. It is usually transparent. Soft-paste porcelain, which is softer and more transparent than the harder variety, is the result of the European potters' unsuccessful attempts to find the formula for true porcelain.

While many English-speaking people refer to porcelain as "china," most Continentals call it porcelain. The clay body of the ware is referred to as "paste," as opposed to the glassy surface, or glaze. Both are fired at the same time, since the materials used in the glaze of hard-paste porcelain are very closely related to those of the paste. It is difficult to detect where one ends and the other begins—especially along the edge of a broken piece of porcelain where they have a tendency to become fused. It is not difficult to identify the glaze as a separate coating on most other kinds of earthenware.

There are three primary ingredients in porcelain. The first is called kaolin, a clay-like material that comprises about 50% of the mixture. It contains varying combinations of aluminum silicates; the latter are difficult to fuse. It is principally white in color, fires white and opaque, and can withstand high temperatures. The second ingredient, called feldspar, forms a fusible glass and acts as a flux under high temperatures; this helps the kaolin to melt and fuse. It comprises about 25% of the mixture, and is usually pinkish or white in color. The last ingredient is quartz. It comprises the remaining 25%. Quartz is the most common solid mineral. The more kaolin used, the harder the porcelain. Different proportions of the ingredients can be used to arrive at the particular texture desired. Thus, the buyer of porcelain will find himself confronted with a wide choice.

Glass

Many different elements are used to make glass. They vary according to the specific type of glass desired. While all glass is clear, hardly any of the elements used in making glass are transparent. The principal element used to make glass is silica sand. It is combined with cullet, the broken or imperfect pieces of glass resulting from the manufacturing process.

Aside from its practical qualities, glass has, since ancient times, enjoyed widespread use throughout the world because of its tremendous beauty. Glass can be decorated in many ways. The ancient Romans, the English, and the Venetians found cutting to be the most effective method for beautifying glass; this is still considered the best procedure. Skilled workmen, using designs that have been placed before them (or ones which were previously stenciled on the glass), make use either of copper wheels supplied with a steady stream of emery dust and oil, or rapidly revolving carborundum wheels of differing sizes. Since such cutting leaves the glass gray, it must subsequently be polished.

Various metals, enamels, and paints are also applied to decorate glass. Silver deposit, gold encrusting, and platinum—which requires a much hotter fire (which in turn requires a special glass capable of withstanding extreme heat)—are among the metal decorations used. Metal-encrusted glassware should be washed only in mild soapsuds, for the use of ammonia or caustic washing powders might dim the metal's polish or cause it to vanish completely. Glass can also be decorated by etching with acid.

If treated properly, fine glassware will remain in good condition indefinitely. Items made of glass should never be rubbed against each other, nor should such pieces be stacked inside one another. Fine glassware can be cleaned by washing it in a mild solution of soapsuds, rinsing it in cool water, and allowing it to dry in a rack. To give glassware a final polish, a lint-free, soft cloth may be used.

"Rock crystal," a term often used in the glass industry, refers to a fine piece of handmade glassware that has been cut and polished. Actually, no glassware is authentic rock crystal, for rock crystal is natural quartz (which, needless to say, can only be created through a natural process). The word "crystal" is used to differentiate fine handmade glass from cheaper, machine-made glass.

Many different mineral salts and oxides are used to color glass. Cobalt oxide, smalt, or jaffre are used to give glass a blue coloration. To make it yellow, cadmium sulphide or uranium are used. Green will result from oxide of chrome, black oxide of copper, or red oxide of iron. Red, one of the costliest colors used, is made from selenium, a substance derived from copper ore. Gold, if added to molten glass, makes glass purple or amber, depending upon the amount of gold added. Ruby glass is also produced by adding gold to a previous mixture.

Higher-priced crystal glass is made by adding lead. This gives the glass a greater resonance, more density, and increases its refractive qualities. Whereas cheaper glass is made with soda ash, fine glass requires potash. Lime, when added to glass, creates an alkali; this gives the glass a greater degree of pliability and strength. Litharge, borax, manganese, arsenic, barium oxide, zinc oxide, alumina, and feldspar are other materials used in the production of glass.

Glass has been used for at least 3,500 years. It was first made in the shape of beads, the form in which it was discovered in the tombs of the Egyptian Kings; it was also fashioned into other decorative shapes. In almost every country that was once a part of the Roman Empire, remains of glass furnaces have been unearthed. Glassmaking was first introduced into Italy. In the Middle Ages the island of Venice became noted for its glass. The craft later spread to Germany and Bohemia.

A glass factory was established in Jamestown, Virginia, in 1608; it marked the birth of America's first industry. Although other factories were subsequently built, the industry did not thrive until a machine to "press" glass into a mold had been invented. A wide variety of glassware—in every conceivable form and color, and using a multiplicity of techniques—was produced by the Boston & Sandwich Glass Company between 1825 (the date Deming Jarves established the firm at Cape Cod) and 1888 (the date it ceased operations).

VII

How a Limited Edition Silver Plate Is Made

Minting began six centuries before Christ, in ancient Lydia, where craftsmen used hand-cut dies to strike coins from soft metal disks. Since then, only two basic innovations have altered the minting process. (1) The introduction of heavy minting presses has increased the force of the minting blow, thus allowing for greater depth of detail. (2) The development of the engraving machine enables a sculptor to work with an object several times larger than its actual size, thus allowing him greater freedom of expression. All other steps in this age-old art have remained essentially unchanged.

Although our federal minting presses turn out as many as five metal-clad coins per second, in the fine art minting process used at private mints every art form—coins, medallions, plates—is slowly proof-minted in precious metal and hand-inspected.

The Sculptor

Before such an object is ready for minting, many creative forces must come into play, starting with the sculptor. He begins by working in clay on a scale two to six times larger than the finished object. When he is satisfied with his design the clay tablet is cast in plaster.

The sculptor   *The engraver*   *Striking*

The sculptor then goes over his work in this harder material. Finally, an even harder epoxy cast is taken from the plaster tablet. Once again the sculptor refines every detail. The epoxy will go to the engraver only when the sculptor is certain that it is as perfect as he can make it.

The Engraver

The epoxy cast now passes into the highly skilled hands of the engraver for the creation of steel minting dies. Perfecting these dies often requires months of handwork and inspection. The mirror-like surface of the final approved die will produce a brilliant "proof finish" on each plate.

Striking

A pure, unmarked sterling silver disk the same size as the plate is first struck between the dies on the minting press and then removed for inspection. A true limited edition plate is always struck in proof finish. Until now, proof finish was limited to only the finest coins and medallions. The Hamilton Mint, where these pictures were taken, was the first to achieve a proof finish on an object as large as a plate; other mints soon followed its example.

232

The hallmark   *The finished plate*

The Minting of Medallions

In addition to collector plates, private mints also make limited edition medallions. A silver planchet is placed on a press to sample-strike new dies. The resulting "test medallion" will be studied to make certain that the dies are perfect.

The Hallmark

To control the quantity of each edition, a collector's serial number is permanently inscribed on the reverse of each art form, together with the Hamilton Mint or other private mint hallmarks, year of issue, and certification of metal content.

When a limited edition is completed, a committee supervises and notarizes the destruction of the dies to protect the integrity of the edition.

The Finished Art Form

After final inspection, each piece is sealed in a protective presentation case, together with an inscribed certificate of authenticity.

VIII

A Glossary of Collectible Plate Terms

Annual: An item issued once each year as part of a series.

Backstamp: Usually appears on the underside of the ware; the name stamp or signature of a manufacturer.

Basalt: Black stoneware which is not glazed.

Bisque: Marble-like, white, unglazed, hard porcelain. Usually·fired twice. Particularly used for making figurines and other intricately detailed designs.

Bone china: China that contains, in addition to refined clays, a percentage of bone ash or its commercial equivalent; this gives it a characteristic whiteness, strength, and translucency (if thin).

Carnival glass: Originally a cheap, decorative glassware developed around the turn of the nineteenth century. It soon became popular as a carnival prize as a result of its unusual iridescent finish. A great deal of higher quality glass with the same type of finish has now gained in popularity among collectors.

Ceramic: Any product which is made with clay, either partly or wholly. It includes everything from the commonest potter's clay to the finest porcelain.

China: Another name for porcelain. A ceramic made of white clay and pulverized stone fired at high temperatures. It will ring clearly when tapped. It is thin, translucent, and resistant to chipping and cracking.

Christmas plates: Many firms produce annual Christmas plates. A producer of plates for export will use the language of the country in which the plates are to be sold, so the same plate may frequently be issued in several different languages. The most common names for Christmas found on plates are: *Jul* and *Julen* for Norway, Sweden, Denmark, Finland, and Iceland; *Noël* for France; *Weihnachten* for Germany, Austria, Switzerland, and other German-speaking countries; *Navidad* for Spain and Portugal; *Natale* for Italy; *Vanoce* for Czechoslovakia; and *Kerstmis* for the Netherlands.

Cobalt blue: The most common type of underglaze coloration. Most of the colors used on unglazed pottery would be destroyed by the high temperature required to glaze a piece of porcelain. Cobalt can withstand the heat very well. It can be used to produce a wide range of blue shades.

Commemorative: An item created to celebrate an event, a place, or to honor an individual.

Crazing: Tiny cracks in the glaze that occur unintentionally when glaze and body contract at different rates.

Crystal: Fine glass which has been given extra weight, better refractive qualities, and a clear ringing tone through the addition of lead. It is called "full lead" crystal when the proportion of lead to glass reaches the level of 24%.

Embossed: A raised or molded decoration, either produced in the mold or formed separately, which is subsequently applied to the body of a piece before firing.

Faience: A heavier type of earthenware, generally possessing a thick glaze. Porcelain, majolica, and delftware fit into this category.

Flow blue: A type of pottery, decorated with cobalt blue, in which the color seems to run outside the design, frequently causing the latter to appear indistinct. The "flowing" occurs unintentionally during the firing of genuine pieces.

Glaze: A liquid, glass-like substance used to cover and seal a piece of porcelain between the first regular-temperature and the second high-temperature firing. It is used to make the surface nonabsorbent, more resistant to wear, as well as for decorative purposes.

Iridescence: A shimmering, rainbow-like finish achieved by spraying the glass with a special formula of acid and metallic salts. It is commonly used on carnival glass.

Jasperware: A hard stoneware requiring no glaze. Developed by Wedgwood and best known in the classic cameo blue and white, it is also made in other colors by other companies.

Limited edition: An item which the manufacturer either produces for a specific period of time or limits in number.

Mint condition: In new or like-new condition; as if freshly minted, like coins.

Mold: A form into which a substance is poured to achieve a certain shape. The mold in ceramic work is usually made of plaster of paris or gypsum. An item can never be duplicated precisely if its mold is lost or destroyed.

Non-limited edition: An item which is usually available for an indefinite period of time or is produced in "open stock."

Overglaze: A design that can be applied after clayware has been fired and glazed. Because they are not subjected to high temperatures, the colors in this decoration tend to be more vivid than those found in underglaze.

Porcelain: A vitreous ware with a transparent glaze. It is fine, white, and translucent. The usual test for porcelain is to hold it up to the light while placing a pencil or your hand behind it; if it is truly porcelain, a shadow will be visible behind it.

Pottery: Clayware which lacks the whiteness, translucency, and hardness of porcelain. The material used for many beautiful pieces of artware, it is more common and easier to work with than porcelain.

Relief: A raised figure or design which stands out from the rest of the background. When it is raised enough to be felt and to emphasize its shape it is called *low relief.* In *high* or *deep relief* the design stands out far enough to create a three-dimensional effect. *Bas-relief* is commonly applied to figures or designs which are slightly deeper than low relief.

Satin finish: The soft frosted look glass acquires when it is dipped into a special acid.

Seconds: Items that are judged by the manufacturer or distributor to be a grade below first quality, often called "second sorting." It is usually indicated by a scratch or gouge through the glaze over the trademark.

Slag: A little bit of a second color added to an opaque glass to form a random, marble-like pattern.

Sterling: The standard of purity for precious metals. In the U.S. it must be 92.5% pure; the exact requirement for sterling silver varies among individual countries.

Transfer: A decal-like print used on china or glass to achieve decoration without handwork. The design was first used in the eighteenth century; it was printed on tissue from copper plates glued to an undecorated item.

Underglaze: A painting or mark applied under the glaze on once-fired porcelain, but before the glazing and second firing.

Special Acknowledgments and Reference Sources

Many people and organizations involved in the production, distribution, and sale of collectible plates were of great help in preparing this book. I am giving their full names and addresses in recognition of their assistance, and as an aid to the reader interested in obtaining further information on the fascinating subject of collectible plates.

Where to Buy and Sell

The dealers listed below generously allowed me to use material from their ads, catalogs, and publications. They are recommended as reliable sources, not only for collectible plates, but for artifacts of all kinds. Some of them are plate importers and distributors as well as dealers, so you will also find their names listed in the section following this one.

Armstrong's, 150 East Third Street, Pomona, Calif. 91767.

Beru's, 4335 Clark Drive, Wanamaker, Ind., 46239.

Bradford Galleries Exchange, 1000 Sunset Ridge Road, Northbrook, Ill. 60062.

Robert G. Burrows, The Burrow Gallerye, 260 Grand Avenue, Englewood, N. J. 07631.

Mrs. Goldstein, David Rubin, My Grandfather's Shop, 8055–13th Street, Silver Spring, Md. 20910.

Bud Kern, Commemorative Imports, Box D, Bayport, Minn. 55003.

Kruckemeyer & Cohn, 410 Main Street, Indianapolis, Ind. 47708.

Pat Owen, Viking Import House, 412 S. E. Sixth Street, Fort Lauderdale, Fla. 33301.

Reese Palley, Reese Palley, Inc., 1911 Boardwalk, Atlantic City, N.J. 08401.

Trein's, 201 W. First, Dixon, Ill. 61021.

Wakefield-Scearce Galleries, Historic Science Hill, Washington Street, Shelbyville, Ky. 40065.

Sylvester A. Wetle, Seven Seas Traders, Inc., Gift Concepts, 415G Belden Avenue, Addison, Ill. 60101.

Plate Importers, Distributors, and Producing Companies

The following individuals and firms have been helpful with information, pricing, and illustrations for the plates in this book. They are recommended as reputable, reliable sources for the plates listed. Inquiries concerning the plates they represent should be sent directly to them at the addresses given.

ADDAMS FAMILY: Matthew F. Schmid, Schmid Brothers, Inc., 55 Pacella Park Drive, Randolph, Mass. 02368.

AMERICA HOUSE/FRANKLIN MINT. See Franklin Mint.

AMERICA THE BEAUTIFUL: E. Ward Russell, The Glass House, P. O. Box 4012, Silver Spring, Md. 20904.

AMERICAN COMMEMORATIVE COUNCIL: Alan Drey, American Commemorative Council, 333 N. Michigan Avenue, Chicago, Ill. 60601.

ANRI: See Addams Family.

ANTIQUE TRADER: E. A. Babka, The Antique Trader, P. O. Box 1050, Dubuque, Iowa 52001.

ARTA: Heio W. Reich, Reco International Corp., 26 South Street, Port Washington, N. Y. 11050.

AYNSLEY CHINA: J. R. Pitts, Aynsley China Ltd., Portland Works, Longton, Stoke-on-Trent, England.

BAREUTHER (see below for Murillo plates): Luella Powell, Walter A. Rautenberg, Wara Intercontinental Co., 20101 West 8 Mile Road, Detroit, Mich. 48219.

BAREUTHER-MURILLO PLATES: Jerry J. Pala, European Crystal, Inc., 212 Fifth Avenue, New York, N. Y. 10010.

BAYEL: George W. Ebeling, Ebeling & Reuss Co., Box 189, 1041 W. Valley Road, Devon, Pa. 19333.

BELLEEK: Belleek China Co. (distributor), 225 Fifth Avenue, New York, N. Y. 10010; Belleek Pottery, Ltd. (producer), County Fermanagh, Ireland.

BERLIN DESIGN: See Addams Family.

BING & GRØNDAHL: Joan Doyle, Bing & Grøndahl Porcelain, Inc., 111 North Lawn Avenue, Elmsford, N. Y. 10523.

BOEHM: See Lenox.

BONITA: Bud Kern, Commemorative Imports, Box D, Bayport, Minn. 55003.

CAPO-DI-MONTE: Koscherak Bros., Inc., 225 Fifth Avenue, New York, N. Y. 10010.

COLLECTOR'S CREATIONS: J. Park Morton, Collector's Creations, P. O. Box 282, Chesterland, Ohio 44026.

COUNT AGAZZI: Pamela Bowman, Count Agazzi of Venice, 349 Peachtree Hills Avenue, N. E. Bldg. C–2, Atlanta, Ga. 30305.

CROWN STAFFORDSHIRE: James P. Kelley, Goebel Art, 250 Clearbroad Road, Elmsford, N. Y.

THE DANBURY MINT: W. Frank Zimmerman, Meta L. Schroeter, The Danbury Mint, Westport, Conn. 06880.

D'ARCEAU-LIMOGES: Ms. Julia Connolly, Bradford Galleries Exchange, 1000 Sunset Ridge Road, Northbrook, Ill. 60062.

DAUM: D. Stanley Corcoran (distributor), 225 Fifth Avenue, New York, N. Y. 10010; P. Cherisey (producer), Daum Cristallerie, 32 Rue de Paradis, 75010 Paris, France.

DELFT
BLUE DELFT: H. Blumner, Blue Delft Company, 1199 Broadway, New York, N. Y. 10001.

BOCH FRÈRES DELFT: See Bayel.

ROYAL DELFT (DE PORCELEYNE FLES): Ivan Glickman, Arista Imports, Rye, N. Y. 10580.

DRESDEN: See Arta.

FENTON ART GLASS: Wilmer C. Fenton, Fenton Art Glass Company, Williamstown, W. Va. 26187.

JUAN FERRANDIZ: See Addams Family.

ALFONSO FONTANA/CREATIVE WORLD: Lee Benson, Veneto Flair/Creative World, 498 Seventh Avenue, New York, N. Y. 10018.

FOSTORIA: David B. Dalzell, Jr., Fostoria Glass Company, Mounsville, W. Va. 26041.

THE FRANKLIN MINT:* David R. Brown, Shirley M. Johnson, The Franklin Mint, Media, Pa. 19063.

FRANKOMA: John Frank, Frankoma Pottery, Box 789, Sapulpa, Okla.

FÜRSTENBERG: See Arta.

THE GEORGE WASHINGTON MINT/MEDALLIC ART COMPANY: Dianne L. Kekessy, Donald A. Schwartz, George Washington Mint/Medallic Art Co., Old Ridgebury Road, Danbury, Conn. 06810.

GORHAM SILVER COMPANY: Ted Materna, Ted Materna Associates (information office), 1350 Avenue of the Americas, New York, N. Y. 10019; The Gorham Company (factory), Providence, R. I. 02907.

GREENTREE/HERITAGE: Joan L. Zug, Greentree Pottery, Heritage Plates, 215 Brown Street, Iowa City, Iowa 52240.

* *The Franklin Mint Museum and Tour.* A unique experience awaits those who take the Franklin Mint's recently initiated two-hour tour. In the mint, you will see how these items are created by skilled craftsmen, and in the museum, a superb collection of medallic art—sculptured coins, medals, and ingots in sterling silver and other precious metals—including a Gallery of Great Americans, Hall of Presidents, Tribute to Nature, and Wonders of the World of Art. The museum is open 9 A.M. to 5 P.M., Monday through Saturday, noon to 5 P.M. on Sunday. Mint tours start every half hour from 9 to 10:30 A.M. and 1 to 3:30 P.M., Monday through Friday. There is no charge for either. To get there: take U.S. Route 1 (south of Media) to Franklin Center, Pa.

GUNTHER GRANGET: Barbara D. Gelinas, Wallace Silversmiths, Wallingford, Conn. 06492.

THE HAMILTON MINT: Tom Rubel, The Hamilton Mint, 40 East University Drive, Arlington Heights, Ill. 60004.

HAVILAND & CO.: Frederick Haviland, Haviland & Co., 11 East 26th Street, New York, N. Y. 10010.

HAVILAND & PARLON: Lloyd Glasgow, Jacques Jugeat, 225 Fifth Avenue, New York, N. Y. 10010.

HUMMEL-GOEBEL, SCHMID: *For Goebel:* James P. Kelly, Hummelwerk, Division of Goebel Art (GmbH), 250 Clearbroad Road, Elmsford, N. Y. 10523. *For Schmid:* See Addams Family.

HUTSCHENREUTHER/TIRSCHENREUTH: W. J. Griffin, B. H. Berman, Hutschenreuther, Ellis Barker Silver Co., Exclusive China Div., 11 East 26th Street, New York, N. Y. 10010.

IMPERIAL GLASS: Lucille Kennedy, Imperial Glass Corp., Bellaire, Ohio 43906.

INTERNATIONAL SILVER COMPANY: Cindy Haskins, International Silver Company, Meriden, Conn. 06450.

ISRAEL CREATIONS: Michael Himelstein, Israel Creations, Inc., 11 West 25th Street, New York, N. Y. 10010.

GEORG JENSEN: Kermit Green, Georg Jensen, 225 Fifth Avenue, New York, N. Y. 10010.

KAISER: Pat Owen, Viking Import House, 412 S. E. Sixth Street, Fort Lauderdale, Fla. 33301.

KING'S PORCELAIN: See Arta.

SAMUEL KIRK: S. Kirk Millspaugh, Sandy Marcus, Samuel Kirk & Sons, Kirk Avenue & 25th Streets, Baltimore, Md. 21218.

KOSTA: See Georg Jensen.

LALIQUE: See Haviland & Parlon.

LENOX: William E. Wedemeyer, Jr., Lenox China, Trenton, N. J. 08605.

THE LINCOLN MINT: Clay Donner, The Lincoln Mint, 1 South Wacker Drive, Chicago, Ill. 60606.

LLADRO: Weil Ceramics & Glass, Inc., 225 Fifth Avenue, New York, N. Y. 10010.

LOURIOUX: See Haviland & Parlon.

LUND & CLAUSEN: Abel Abrahamsen, Norsk, 114 East 57th Street, New York, N. Y. 10022.

KAY MALLEK: Kay Mallek, 1208 N. Alvernon Way, Tucson, Ariz. 85712.

MARMOT: See Arta.

METAWA: See Addams Family.

METLOX: Doug Bothwell, Metlox Potteries, Manhattan Beach, Calif. 90266.

MOSER: See Arta.
MUELLER, WUERFUL/SCHMID: See Addams Family.

NIDAROS: See Lund & Clausen.

ORREFORS: R. MacDonald, Fisher-Bruce & Co., 221 Market Street, Philadelphia, Pa. 19106.

PEANUTS: See Addams Family.
PICKARD: Henry A. Pickard, Pickard Inc., Antioch, Ill. 60002.
GILBERT POILLERAT/CRISTAL D'ALBRET: Paul Jokelson, P. O. Box 128, Scarsdale, N. Y. 10583.
POOLE POTTERY, LTD.: See Hutschenreuther/Tirschenreuth.
PORCELAIN DE PARIS: See Hutschenreuther/Tirschenreuth.
PORSGRUND: See Lund & Clausen.
PUIFORCAT: Anthony H. Clipper, Puiforcat U. S. A., 225 Fifth Avenue, New York, N. Y. 10010.

REED & BARTON: Stafford P. Osborn, Reed & Barton, Taunton, Mass. 02780.
RORSTRAND: See Orrefors.
ROSENTHAL: Peter Meltzer, Rosenthal/Studio Haus, 584 Fifth Avenue, New York, N. Y. 10036.
ROYAL BAYREUTH: Daniel M. Price, H. Wittur & Co., 1024–1026 Emerson Street, Evanston, Ill. 60204.
ROYAL COPENHAGEN: See Kaiser.
ROYAL DOULTON: Nancy E. O. Clarke, Royal Doulton & Co., 400 Paterson Plank Road, Carlstadt, N. J. 07072.
ROYAL IRISH SILVER LTD.: Peter H. Gunning, Royal Irish Limited, 30 Dublin Industrial Estate, Finglas, Dublin, Ireland.
ROYAL TETTAU: See Royal Bayreuth.
ROYALE/GERMANIA CRYSTAL: Dorothy George, Reco International Corp., 26 South Street, Port Washington, N. Y. 11050.

SCHUMANN: See Bayel.
SEVEN SEAS TRADERS: Sylvester A. Wetle, Seven Seas Traders, Inc., Gift Concepts, 415G Belden Avenue, Addison, Ill. 60101.
SILVER CITY: See Bonita.
SILVER CREATIONS: I. Moscow, Silver Creations, 428 Old Hook Road, Emerson, N. J.
L. E. SMITH GLASS/WENDELL AUGUST FORGE: Hank Opperman, L. E. Smith Glass Co., P. O. Box 149, Mount Pleasant, Pa. 15666.
SPODE: Barbara Deutsch, Spode, Inc., Turnpike Industrial Park, 26 Kennedy Boulevard, East Brunswick, N. J. 08816.

ST. AMAND: Porcelain St. Amand, St. Amand, France.

FRANZ STANEK/WARA INTERCONTINENTAL: See Bareuther.

STERLING AMERICA/SILVER CITY: See Bonita.

STUMAR: Sid Sachs, Stumar/Glenview Pottery, 2650 West Maple Avenue, Langhorne, Pa. 19047.

SVEND-JENSEN/DÉSIRÉE: Erik Larsen, Svend-Jensen of Denmark, 1010 Boston Post Road, Rye, N. Y. 10580.

VAL SAINT LAMBERT: H. Schulte, William Adams, Inc., 208 Fifth Avenue, New York, N. Y. 10010.

VAN GOGH/CREATIVE WORLD: See Alfonso Fontana/Creative World.

VENETO FLAIR/CREATIVE WORLD: See Alfonso Fontana/Creative World.

WEDGWOOD: A. J. Pointon, Claudia Coleman, Wedgwood, 555 Madison Avenue, New York, N. Y. 10022.

THE WELLINGS MINT/FRANKLIN MINT: See America House.

WHEATON/NULINE GLASS: John F. Heiner, Wheaton Industries, Millville, N. J. 08332.

WILTON ARMETALE: Jack Fitzpatrick, Wilton Armetale, Columbia, Pa. 17512.

Trade Missions, Embassies, and Consulates

The personnel of the embassies, trade consulates, and commercial missions of the following plate-producing countries were of great assistance. They possess considerable information which can be made available to interested individuals.

BELGIUM: Mr. A. Van Oppens, Executive Secretary, The Belgian-American Chamber of Commerce in the U. S., Inc., 50 Rockefeller Plaza, New York, N. Y. 10020.

DENMARK: Mr. Jens Pallesen, Commercial Secretary, Consulate General of Denmark, 280 Park Avenue, New York, N. Y. 10017.

FRANCE: Mr. Pierre Weill, The Commercial Counselor, The French Embassy, 1301 Avenue of the Americas, New York, N. Y. 10019.

GERMANY: Mrs. R. Haab, German-American Chamber of Commerce, 666 Fifth Avenue, New York, N. Y. 10019.

GREAT BRITAIN: Commercial Attaché, British Trade Development Office, 150 East 58th Street, New York, N. Y. 10019.

HOLLAND: Mr. J. Martin Bakels, Executive Secretary, Chamber of Commerce in the U. S., Inc., 1 Rockefeller Plaza, New York, N. Y. 10020.

ITALY: Mr. Lucio Caputo, Italian Trade Commissioner, World Trade Center, New York, N. Y. 10048.

Magazines and Newspapers

The following publications will prove helpful to collectors, dealers, or anyone interested in plates of all types. They can be ordered by mail, either in individual issues or by subscription. (Several publications offer a free trial issue.) They are also excellent sources to buy, sell, or trade plates.

NEWSPAPERS

Antique Monthly, P. O. Drawer 440, Tuscaloosa, Ala. 35401.
Antique News, Box B, Marietta, Pa. 17547.
Antique Trader, Box 1050, Dubuque, Iowa 52001.
Collector's News, Box 156, Grundy Center, Iowa 50638.
Collector's Weekly, Box 1119, Kermit, Tex. 79745.
Plate Collector, P. O. Box 1041, Kermit, Tex. 79745.
Tri-State Trader, P. O. Box 90-DM, Knighstown, Ind. 46148.

MAGAZINES

The foremost magazine published today on the subject of contemporary collectibles is, in our opinion, *Acquire* magazine. It contains much information (plus illustrations) on the subject of plate production and collecting. It can be ordered by writing to the following address:

Acquire, 170 Fifth Avenue, New York, N. Y. 10010.

Other magazines containing articles on plates and related subjects are:

Antiques Journal, Babka Publishing Co., Kewanee, Ill. 61443.
China Glass & Tablewares, 1115 Clifton Avenue, Clifton, N. J. 07103.
The Classic Collector, 711 S. Saint Asaph St., Alexandria, Va. 22314.
Eastern Antiquity, 1 Dogwood Drive, Washington, N. J. 07882.
Gifts & Decorative Accessories, Geyer-McAllister Publications, 51 Madison Ave., New York, N. Y. 10010.
Hobbies, Lightner Publishing Corp., 1006 S. Michigan Ave., Chicago, Ill. 60605.
National Antiques Review, P. O. Box 619, Portland, Me. 04104.
Relics, P. O. Box 3668, 1012 Edgecliff Terrace, Austin, Tex. 78704.
Silver, 1619-A S.W. Jefferson St., Portland, Ore. 97201.
Spinning Wheel, Everybodys Press, Inc., Hanover, Pa. 17331.
Treasure, 7950 Deering Ave., Canoga Park, Calif. 91304.
Western Antique Mart, P. O. Box 2171, Eugene, Ore. 97402.
Western Collector, P. O. Box 9166, San Francisco, Calif. 94129.

Bibliography

HOTCHKISS, JOHN F. *Limited Edition Collectibles.* 1974. $5.95. Hawthorn Books, Inc.

NEWMAN, EARL N. *The Danish Royal Copenhagen Plaquettes—2010 Series.* $6.95. (Available from Viking Import House, 412 S. E. Sixth Street, Fort Lauderdale, Fla. 33301.)

OWEN, PAT. *The Story of Bing & Grøndahl Christmas Plates.* 1962. $8.00. (Available from author at above address.)

OWEN, PAT. *The Story of Royal Copenhagen Christmas Plates.* 1962. $8.00. (Available from author at above address.)

STEINKE, VIOLETTE. *Original Royal Delft Christmas Plates.* 1972. $10.00. Gray Printing Co., Birmingham, Ala.

WITT, LOUISE SCHAUB. *The Wonderful World of Plates.* 1970 (and supplements). $12.50. (Available from author at: K & L Publications, Box 38, Shawnee Mission, Shawnee, Kans. 66201.)